Published in 2016 by Universe Press,
an imprint of Unicorn Publishing Group

101 Wardour Street
London.
W1F 0UG

ISBN 978-0-993242-48-9

10 9 8 7 6 5 4 3 2 1

Front cover designed by Felicity Price-Smith

Interior designed by Maisie Franklin

Printed in Spain at GraphyCems

WELLINGTON'S
Dearest Georgy

THE LIFE AND LOVES OF LADY GEORGIANA LENNOX

ALICE MARIE CROSSLAND

WITH A FOREWORD BY
LORD DE ROS

FOREWORD

BY PETER MAXWELL 28TH BARON DE ROS

Last winter, with the 200th anniversary of the Battle of Waterloo approaching, I took to reading through the many letters that passed between my ancestor Lady Georgiana Lennox, later Lady de Ros, and the 1st Duke of Wellington. I was struck by their very deep affection for each other and the fascinating period of time in which they lived.

Having lived most of my life here in Strangford, alongside the lough and its beautiful surroundings, there is still a very strong feeling of Georgy's influence here. The older parts of the garden are still laid out and landscaped as Georgy and William, her devoted husband, planned them.

I was introduced to Alice whilst she was researching the miniature given to Georgiana at the ball hosted by her mother, the Duchess of Richmond, the night before the Battle of Waterloo. Alice's interest in Wellington, her enthusiasm and passion for the subject, was very obvious from the outset, so I invited her to come and see the collection of memorabilia and letters which are still in my family's possession. Her book is the result of three years of meticulous researching and writing.

Alice spent many weekends here in Strangford, where Georgiana is buried, painstakingly piecing together the story of her life and loves and particularly her extraordinary friendship with the Duke of Wellington. The result has brought Georgiana to life for me, as I am sure it will for many others, in this charming and enthralling book.

To Peter and Sian Maxwell,

who introduced me to Georgy's story and who welcomed me so warmly into their home.

CONTENTS

INTRODUCTION

Lady Georgiana Lennox was born on a perfectly ordinary Wednesday in 1795. As the fifth child in a rapidly growing family her birth passed without much fanfare. Her four elder brothers and sisters had already been passed on to an army of nurses, to be observed at tea time by Georgy's beady-eyed mother, the future Duchess of Richmond. Over the years Georgiana, or Georgy as she was known to her closest friends and family, watched through wide eyes the arrival of nine more siblings. Each birth passed by Georgy's parents without much alteration to their socialising and sporting regime. Such was the way for most eighteenth-century aristocratic families. Each Lennox baby grew healthy and strong, largely ignored by their mother and doted upon by their father. So begins the story of Georgy Lennox; for despite the fact that Georgy would become neither extremely famous nor wealthy, her story is entwined with that of one of the most celebrated men in British history: the 1st Duke of Wellington.

Moving through Europe in her teens Georgy was witness to some of the most significant moments of the nineteenth century. She had a front row seat to the events in Brussels in June 1815, when Napoleon Bonaparte escaped from exile and marched towards an Allied Army, with Wellington its Commander-in-Chief. The resultant Battle of Waterloo is arguably the most famous battle in British history, securing a lasting peace with France. Georgy and the Iron Duke, as he later became known, were close friends in the years before and after the battle and the true nature and intimacy of their relationship has long been disputed.

Why Georgy's story is not more widely known remains to be fully determined. She never gained the heights of celebrity like Marianne Patterson or Harriet Arbuthnot, two other of 'Wellington's Women', despite the fact that she and Wellington enjoyed forty-six years of friendship together. He was an influential part of Georgy's life and clearly cared for her very deeply. Georgy herself was certainly besotted with the Duke from a young age and recorded much of their meetings and her thoughts about him in a diary throughout her life. After her death however, her diary was destroyed by her daughter Blanche, after she had transcribed small fragments from it over the years. Also gone were many of her more personal keepsakes which had been preserved in loving memory of a man that she treasured as much as any member of her own family. Wellington in turn destroyed every single one of Georgy's letters to him, in an attempt to cover up the intimacy of their friendship.

However, by working through public and private records, letters and artefacts, the story of Georgy Lennox and the Duke of Wellington has now been pieced back together again and can be told in full for the first time.

CHAPTER ONE

The Great Sir Arthur

'Genl Lennox...is a most friendly man, perfectly free from pride, but the Dss [Duchess] is of an opposite disposition being excessively proud and disdainful of persons of inferior rank'.[1]

The diarist Joseph Farington on the 4th Duke and Duchess of Richmond

Georgy was born into the dynastic Lennox family that made up the Duchy of Richmond, Lennox and Aubigny. The 1st Duke of Richmond had been the natural son of Charles II and his glamorous French mistress Louise de Kérouaille, Duchess of Portsmouth. The Richmonds' principal estate was Goodwood House in Sussex and they also had a palatial home in Whitehall, London. By end of the eighteenth century the Richmond family was second perhaps only to the Royal Family in terms of social influence and power. They lived in some of the most luxurious and fashionable abodes, travelled widely, and befriended or married into other upper class families. At the many balls and soirées the Lennoxes attended, they mingled with other aristocrats and society figures, safe in a gilded world of luxury and privilege.

Georgy's father Charles Lennox was the son of Lord George Lennox, nephew of the 3rd Duke of Richmond and Lady Louisa Kerr, daughter of the 4th Marquis of Lothian. Charles Lennox was extremely popular amongst his family and his peers. He was a keen sportsman with a special love for the game of cricket, which had become universally popular through the efforts of his grandfather the 2nd Duke of Richmond. As a young man Charles took his place in the Army and soon gained a reputation as a fun-loving and headstrong young buck.

In 1789, in the space of two short months, Charles Lennox fought two duels. In eighteenth-century English society, this was considered the gentlemanly way of settling a dispute. Each participant was provided with a pair of pistols and chose a 'second' to step in if they were mortally wounded. Each man was allowed a single shot and could decide whether or not they aimed to kill. Charles's first duel was held on Wimbledon Common, and was against none other than the Duke of York, King George III's second and favourite son, and also Charles's Commanding Officer. Charles was an excellent shot, and the Duke of York had a narrow escape when the bullet shot off one of the curls on his wig.[2] The Duke's own pistol failed to fire. Whether Charles's action had been extremely brave or extremely stupid was discussed at length by the gossip-loving London society, and the incident certainly sealed his reputation as a man of action who would go far. Only two months after this extraordinary event, Charles Lennox fought another duel against a man who had published a pamphlet that slurred his character. Theophilus Swift was hit in the body by Charles's shot, but the injury did not prove fatal. The details of these legendary duels were often told by Charles to his children, many years later, who would grow up idolising their brave and daring Papa.

1789 was also the year that Charles Lennox's younger sister Georgiana married Lord Apsley who became the 3rd Earl Bathurst the following year. Lord Bathurst would go on to provide support to the Duke of Wellington during the Peninsular War as Secretary for War and the Colonies. Lady Bathurst became close to her many nieces and nephews over the years, and played an especially important part in the upbringing of little Georgy, her namesake. Together Lord and Lady Bathurst built Apsley House, a grand Robert Adam mansion on the corner of Hyde Park in London. The house would later become famous as Wellington's principal abode.

Meanwhile Charles Lennox quickly gained promotion through the ranks. He was popular with his men, particularly as he allowed them to beat him at cricket. He was handsome and charming and heir to one of the most prestigious titles in the land, so women attached themselves to him in droves and few of their advances were spurned. When Charles went with his regiment to Edinburgh he stayed with the Duke and Duchess of Gordon, who belonged to one of the oldest land owning dynasties in Scotland. Charles had met their beautiful and haughty daughter Charlotte during the London season and they quickly became reacquainted. The Duchess of Gordon was a leading

Tory hostess, she was a rather overbearing character who had great ambitions for her five beautiful daughters. Her grandson recalled:

> 'Her personal graces she transmitted...to her daughters, five in number, who became severally the belles of their season; indeed for many years after the single blessedness of their career had terminated, when they appeared together at the opera, or theatre, in the same box as their mother...their extraordinary attractiveness became the source of universal admiration'.[3]

Charles was just the sort of match the Duchess intended for her daughters, and she marked him out as such soon after his arrival. It was after just five days of staying at Gordon Castle that the Duchess successfully brought about a union between Charles and Charlotte. The wedding ceremony took place in the Duchess's dressing room and the only witnesses were the Duchess herself and two of her maids. The marriage, rather mysteriously, was kept secret from everyone else for a further two days. When it was finally announced, the Duchess was universally congratulated on having achieved such a fine match and creating a lasting union between two of Britain's most ancient and noble families. In the end all of the Duchess of Gordon's daughters acquired fine titles: Charlotte became the Duchess of Richmond and her sisters included the future Lady Sinclair, the Duchess of Manchester, and the Marchioness Cornwallis.

Charlotte shared many of her mother's characteristics: she was proud and demanding and loved partying, shopping and gambling. She did not possess, however, the charm and easy manners of her new husband. Her haughty nature did not endear her to friends, and she was above all a capricious snob. There was one attribute however that

Charles's new wife did hold in abundance, and that was her ability to bear healthy children at impressively regular intervals. Between the years 1791-1809 she had fourteen children: seven boys and seven girls. First to come was Charles who was later known by his courtesy title March, after his father became the Duke of Richmond. March was followed by Mary, John and then Sarah. Georgiana, or Georgy, was born in 1795 and two years following this her brother Henry was born. Two years later in 1799 came Lord William Pitt Lennox, who like Georgy would later publish his own recollections of life as a Lennox. The following year Jane was born, and the year after that Frederick. In 1802 Sussex joined the nursery, who was followed in a routine sort of way by Louisa, Charlotte, Arthur and then finally in 1809, Sophia. Georgy's mother continued to socialise extensively during and in between each pregnancy and showed little sign of fatigue from the effect of having so many babies in such a short space of time. In the tradition of aristocratic motherhood, she remained largely distant from her children until they reached a marriageable age, however she doted on March as her son and heir.

Throughout the early years of their marriage the Lennoxes lived at Molecomb, the dowager house on the Goodwood estate, creating a precedent for all future Richmond heirs. Life at Molecomb was idyllic for the young Georgy Lennox. The children were not kept confined to their lessons, and were more likely to be 'found in the stable rather than the schoolroom',[4] roaming free over the vast estate around Goodwood House. One of Georgy's earliest memories was going over to the big house to play with her pretty cousin Lady Pamela Fitzgerald, daughter of the disgraced Irish revolutionary Lord Edward Fitzgerald. In 1789 Edward Fitzgerald had been hunted down by the authorities

1. Molecomb House on the Goodwood estate where Georgy and her siblings spent their early years. Image author's own.

on charges of inciting revolution in Ireland, and died whilst in prison from injuries sustained during the arrest; thus making him a martyr for the Irish republican cause. Pamela had been smuggled over from France in a cheese ship and her Lennox cousins greatly envied her French coal-scuttle shaped bonnet. Another of Georgy's play fellows was Princess Charlotte, only daughter of the Prince Regent and his estranged wife Princess Caroline. Georgy later described the universally beloved princess as a 'merry, frank and extremely indiscreet girl, openly avowing that the two things in the world she most hated were "boiled mutton and grandmamma!"'[5]

When she was nine Georgy's father succeeded his uncle to the title of Duke of Richmond. Initially the family moved into Goodwood House which had recently been expanded at great cost. However, inheriting debt from his uncle to the tune of £180,000 (some £8,000,000 in today's money), the new Duke found himself in a difficult position. Living at Goodwood became increasingly unrealistic and he needed a steady income. Luckily the Duke and Duchess could draw on their many influential friends, including the Prime Minister William Pitt. When Pitt came to supper the children would be summoned to the dining room to meet the great man. He even lent his name to his godson William Pitt Lennox, one of Georgy's brothers. Pitt did what he could for the family but died in 1806 soon after Charles became the Duke of Richmond. However, under the new government formed by the ailing Duke of Portland came the possibility of new political appointments. Richmond was in need of a position which would bring in much needed capital and it was Lord Bathurst who helped him to get the important and influential position of Lord Lieutenant of Ireland. At the time the position boasted an annual salary of £20,000, and was deemed an appropriately grand occupation for such a member of the establishment. However, Richmond still needed to make a raft of economies to save his family from ruin. The Duke took the decision to close up Goodwood House and move his whole family to Dublin. With his escalating financial troubles he had little choice.

The family left for Dublin in April 1807 and soon settled into their new life across the Irish sea. The Duchess was thrilled by the glamour of her new position where she was able to reign over her own miniature court of officials, attendees and foreign visitors. The family were soon introduced to the young and charming Colonel Arthur Wellesley who held the position of Chief Secretary of Ireland under the Duke of Richmond.

Arthur Wesley (the family name was changed back to its anglicised version of Wellesley in 1798) was the third son of the Earl and Countess of Mornington, a minor Anglo-Irish land-owning family who had a small estate in County Meath, Ireland. As a young boy Arthur was not considered particularly bright or promising, indeed he was often overshadowed by the academic brilliance of his eldest brother Richard. Arthur spent a few terms at Eton but was removed as his family did not consider him to be making much of an improvement and like the Richmonds, the Wellesleys were having financial problems. As a young man Arthur had met and fallen in love with the beautiful and charming Kitty Pakenham, the daughter of a neighbouring aristocratic family. Kitty was the darling of Dublin's, admittedly limited, social scene. She had many potential suitors who viewed her quiet charm and fine features with interest. Arthur's request for her hand was twice refused by Kitty's family as they did not think his prospects good enough to support their daughter to the standard they expected. Arthur was devastated by this rejection of both his person and his social status, and from this time onwards worked hard to prove his worth in his chosen field of occupation: the Army. His hope was to prove himself to his family and to Kitty's, and to return from his soldiering with enough fortune and prospects to convince Kitty's family of his marital worth.

In 1796 Arthur's regiment made plans to serve in India. He assured Kitty that if her family's opposition to the match should change, his desire to marry her would remain unaltered. Over the next few years, Arthur and his brother Richard, who was then Governor-General of India, worked tirelessly to secure Southern India against the French. When they returned to England in September 1805, Arthur's exploits had gained him widespread fame. He had been promoted to Major

General and knighted for his services to the crown and so returned as Major General Sir Arthur Wellesley, having amassed an impressive fortune of £42,000. In addition, thanks to the expanding print press industry and the dissemination of prints based on portraits by Robert Home and a bust by the eminent Joseph Nollekens, his name and image were now well known.

Arthur had been in India for eight years straight, and had had limited contact with his Irish acquaintances during that time. On his return and to everyone's surprise he immediately renewed his suit to Kitty, despite the fact that he had neither seen nor written to her since he had left for India. Kitty had remained deeply devoted to Arthur but over the years the innocent beauty who had so entranced him as a young man had diminished. She had suffered with her health and become a plain and withdrawn woman, no longer in the prime of her youth. One friend confirmed 'she is now thin and withered (I believe pining in his absence helped to make her more so).'[6]

Still the marriage offer was renewed and accepted but Arthur did not see Kitty until a few days before their wedding, which took place on 10th April 1806. Supposedly he whispered to his brother Gerald, who was to marry them: 'She has grown ugly, by jove!'[7] Despite this the marriage began well, and Kitty bore two sons in quick succession. They became the central objects of her life as she tried to build a relationship with their father. However, it quickly became apparent that the two were not well matched. Kitty idolised her husband, and when they differed his sharp retorts upset her, making her timid. In turn Arthur found Kitty's quiet nature an irritant and her attentions suffocating. Despite her shyness, Kitty could hold her ground in arguments and was often stubborn to the point of exasperation. Arthur had an impatient temper and did not suffer fools gladly. In his personal life he was used to acting in his own interest, he had never before had to make himself accountable to a woman. Often separated by her husband's work, Kitty would be left in London with their two sons, Arthur and Charles, and soon the emotional distance between them was too big a gap to bridge. Their relationship was quickly reduced to letters regarding household issues. When Arthur did return to London, Kitty did not fulfil her role as the wife of a military hero as he expected. At balls and evening events they attended together, Kitty would refuse to dress as the other ladies, eschewing diamonds for her favourite cheap garnets and insisting on wearing simple gowns that had been acceptable back in Dublin. She lacked the confidence to endure these social commitments with the easy grace shown by Arthur's newly forming band of female admirers, who were, by contrast, urbane and sophisticated. Provincial Kitty felt that she could not compete and so removed herself from the competition. Soon she rarely attended such events.

A year after their marriage Arthur was appointed Chief Secretary in Ireland and the young Wellesley family relocated to Dublin. Kitty was thrilled to be returning to the country where she had grown up, away from the social pressures of life in London. Soon they were joined by the ever-growing Richmond clan who took over the Lord Lieutenant's residence in Phoenix Park. Arthur was not able to spend a great deal of time in Dublin during this period, leaving for a few months to lead an expedition to Copenhagen. The following year he would be summoned to even greater fame and fortune in Portugal, where he would battle Napoleon's forces. However, during the six months or so that he and Kitty spent in Dublin, they both became close to the Duke and Duchess of Richmond. The Duchess in particular was able to comfort Kitty as she was quite used to the marital hiccups that accompanied the early years of such a union, where neither party had had the chance to acquaint themselves with each other properly before marrying. Both Wellesley children were baptised in Dublin with the whole Lennox clan in attendance, and the Duke of Richmond was made Charles's godfather.

Whilst the Duke and Duchess travelled extensively around Ireland socialising and visiting local people in an attempt to subdue rising religious tensions, Georgy and her many siblings were left to the care of a governess. Georgy took her lessons, daily walks and dancing classes in the peace and tranquillity of Phoenix Park. The younger Lennox boys had been dispatched to Westminster School in London but thoroughly enjoyed their holidays spent back in Ireland. As Arthur and his wife grew further apart he found himself growing closer to the Richmond family and was quick to make an impression on the young Lennox girls. Having returned from India suntanned and still with the fine features of his youth including his ever-recognisable hooked nose, he was easily the most attractive man they knew. Their easy and uncomplicated company appealed to Arthur's carefree nature and soon he became a regular visitor.

The Richmond children were often present at the many dinners and balls which made up the official social calendar of Richmond's Lord Lieutenancy. The Duke had a great love for parties and was a seasoned drinker. He welcomed anyone to his table with the same attitude, indeed 'any harmless frolic was sanctioned'[8] in the Richmond household. Like many husbands of the time the Duke of Richmond conducted affairs outside of the marital bed, seeking relief from his difficult (and invariably pregnant) wife. He openly courted the beautiful Lady Augusta Somerset and it was to Augusta that Richmond wrote a late night love letter which was mistakenly delivered to his extremely irate wife, who subsequently brought the house down with her raging. The Duchess was forced to endure further humiliation when the Duke insisted that Augusta dine with the family every day. The Duke's lover supposedly claimed rather proudly that she thought 'The Old Puss will burst with jealousy'.

The following year the Duke and Duchess took a selection of their daughters to see the first night of the theatre production *The Country Girl*, starring the celebrated Mrs Jordan. Mrs Jordan was almost as famous for her acting as she was for being the Duke of Clarence's mistress. She was rather shocked to receive a sexual proposition from Georgy's father that evening. He had been enthralled with her performance and wrote seeking a private meeting. Mrs Jordan rather haughtily declined his request and Richmond was left unsatisfied.

The Duke's ebullient character shone through in his relationship with his offspring who all adored him. Life in Ireland was proving to be just as fun and carefree for them as it had been in England. During the Christmas holidays the younger boys travelled back from Westminster School to Dublin. After a harrowing and exhausting journey across the rough Irish sea they relished being back with their family and particularly spending time with their father. William later wrote:

> 'The delights of these holidays cannot easily be described. I and my brother accompanied my father in his shooting expeditions; and daily enjoyed the luxuries of a good dessert and a glass of wine. We were taken to all the sights in the metropolis...to the plains of Curragh; the waters of the Avoca; the falls of Powerscourt; and last, not least, in our estimation, we

> attended the theatre on the night of the Viceroyal "Bespeak," and were allowed to go there on numerous other occasions."[9]

Arthur Wellesley revelled in the noise, the bustle and the frivolity of the Richmond family. He and Georgy enjoyed each other's company immensely, sharing a sharp-witted sense of humour. Despite their twenty-six year age gap, Georgy was confident and boisterous enough to chat with Arthur with ease. In turn, he felt he could relax around Georgy and her sisters, laughing and sharing jokes. Georgy later recounted: '…we saw a great deal of him. My sisters and I used to ride with "great Sir Arthur" as we called him, every day from the Vice-Regal Lodge in the Phoenix Park to the Dublin Gate, when he was going to his office.'[10]

Georgy undoubtedly idolised Arthur, and he can easily be seen as her first teenage 'crush'. In his own way Arthur was attracted by the innocent enthusiasm of the young Georgy Lennox. Although there has always been some conjecture as to the true extent of their relationship, the friendly roots put down in those early days in Dublin suggests at this stage only a mutual affection and friendship. Georgy adored their daily rituals of hacking out together and often recalled these rides later in life.

As well as the small gifts and tokens that Arthur bestowed on the Richmond children, he also promised support for them in the future. He cared for them all and took their interests seriously. During one evening's entertainment William Pitt Lennox and some of his brothers put on a rather botched amateur production in fancy dress, which delighted Arthur who described it as 'Capital! Capital!' Later calling William over, he exclaimed playfully to the Duchess 'You had better send them to Covent Garden or Sadler's Wells [both famous theatres] 'to which the Duchess responded:

> 'I hope better things for him...he desires a commission in the army'
>
> 'Well, we'll see what can be done, how old is he?'
>
> 'Just eight'
>
> 'Plenty of time before him' Wellesley mused, but did not forget his word.

The never-ending calendar of dinners, parties and evening entertainments meant that Richmond did not find life in Dublin as economical as he had hoped. Despite an increase in his annual salary by £10,000 the family was still heavily in debt. In 1809 Wellesley returned to the Peninsular campaign to push Napoleon's forces out of Spain. Napoleon was gaining ground by the month and Arthur was anxious to get back to the battlefield where he was now confident that he could make a real difference. Richmond did not wish to see such a competent and charming official leave his court but understood Arthur's desire to further prove himself on the military stage. It was a desire he too shared, tied down as he was by his ceremonial role in Ireland. No-one, Richmond included, wanted to see any more European land being claimed in the name of the Emperor Napoleon. Everyone wished him farewell and good luck, especially the Lennox sisters who so doted on him. They were sad to see their 'Great Sir Arthur' go.

Life in Dublin continued in much the same way even without Arthur. The Lennox family, an outpost for the English court and everything it stood for, were surprisingly well liked by the local community, despite continued political tensions across the country. In October of that year everyone rushed out into the streets of Dublin to see the illuminations that heralded the Jubilee celebrations of King George III. Georgy wore a sash with 'God save the King' on it. William Ogilvie, who happened to be the second husband of Georgy's future grandmother-in-law, was with the group and recalled going:

> 'with some of the young Ladies [Georgy included] and the Duchess to see the Illuminations, which far exceeded anything I ever saw in London or Paris. Nothing ever equalled the Brilliancy of the Illuminations- I do not believe there was a Window in this Great City that was not illuminated down to the Cobbler's Stall and the Variety and fancy of the Transparent pencillings was very great- and had a fine effect. The Crowds in the Streets exceeded everything I could have conceived, but the most perfect good humour reigned thro' them all, and I have not heard of a single Accident. The Duke and Duchess who passed from the Park to Stephens Green to see Fire-Works were everywhere huzza-ed and applauded by the People'[11]

It was true that the Richmonds continued to be very popular with the Irish people. Ogilvie continued 'No Lord-Lieut. ever reigned so much in the Hearts of the People…He understands them and manages them beyond any Body I ever saw- and the Dutchess [sic] is also a very great favourite.'[12]

Three years later in 1813 Richmond's tenure as Lord Lieutenant of Ireland came to an end and the whole family moved back to London. The grand and imposing Richmond House in Whitehall, which had for so long housed generations of Lennoxes, lay in ruins after a devastating fire so the family moved into an adjacent house which the Duke had purchased. Despite still being in serious financial difficulties, the Richmonds also returned to Goodwood House. Georgy and her siblings were now under the watchful eye of a rather stern Swiss governess but within a few months they would be escorted into the London social scene by their mother who was intent on finding each of them a husband. The Duchess, like her mother before her, understood the importance of good matches for her daughters. From this time onwards she took a more active role in the discipline and education of her seven daughters, ensuring their conversation, posture and comportment were fine-tuned, ready for any potential suitors.

The same year that they arrived in London the Duchess and all of her daughters were presented at Court, the annual formal entry of upper class ladies into 'Society'. They arrived in the grandest of styles, each in their own sedan chair and attended by a running footman. Sarah, the second eldest Lennox daughter 'came out' that year; meaning that she was formally introduced to 'The Season', where she could expect to find a husband. At this time, it was customary for daughters of high ranking aristocrats to be presented privately to the Monarch in the evening rather than during the main ceremony. Sarah's name was presented on arrival, but the King's officials sent back the card with a request: if the young lady had another name could that possibly be used instead? The reason for this rather curious request was that Sarah shared her name with her great aunt, the notorious sister of the 3rd Duke of Richmond. This Sarah Lennox had been an early lover of George III's when he had been the Prince of Wales. It was thought that the very mention of the name might upset the poor blind monarch. Sarah unfortunately had no other name to use. When she was finally presented to the King, to her 'great surprise and consternation' he begged to be able to feel her features, knowing that Sarah and her great-aunt looked alike. Sarah was not much pleased, but 'said she could not refuse, knowing the reason of the request, but she found it a very embarrassing position.'[13]

Whilst life had continued in a familiar way for the Richmonds, Arthur had endured a very different set of experiences. In August 1809 he had landed in Portugal with a force of 9,000 men. After fighting the Battles of Rolica and Vimiero, the British had their victory; and owed much of it to the efforts of Sir Arthur Wellesley. Unfortunately, this was not to be a lasting peace as the excessively lenient Convention of Cintra allowed the French to return home in British ships with their booty intact. Arthur and the two other commanders who had signed this ill-fated document were recalled to England for an enquiry, but Arthur was quickly vindicated. The full extent of this disastrous move quickly became apparent as within weeks Napoleon had invaded Spain with 200,000 men and soon occupied Madrid. Arthur returned to the peninsular in April, confident that he could now hold Portugal against the French. As reward for his services he was made Viscount Wellington of Talavera and Kitty became Lady Wellington.

Lord March, Georgy's eldest brother, joined the army as soon as he was deemed old enough and was Wellington's Assistant Military Secretary and Aide-de-Camp from 1810-14. March quickly became one of the Duke's most liked and trusted staff officers. He was severely injured in February 1814 at the Battle of Orthez, the final clash with the French before Napoleon was forced to abdicate. Easily her favourite brother, Georgy kept a report of March's injuries in her family's archive:

> 'Lord March was taken to Orthez to a house that was made into a Hospital- the following night he was great danger, & Dr. Hare 43rd gave strict orders that he should be kept as quiet as possible- He sat up with him all night- & towards the middle of the night the door opened, & a figure walked up to the bed drew back the curtain & leaning over Ld March kissed his forehead & with a sigh left the room, & the Dr saw it was Wellington, who had riden [sic] many miles alone that night to see the son of his great friend, & one of his favourite A.D.C.'s. He returned to headquarters after having made enquiries & given orders about the sick & wounded & sent Lord George Lennox to look after his brother'.[14]

The doctor reported to Wellington that the ball had entered March's body three inches below the armpit and had lodged behind the shoulder blade. Another letter from Wellington gave further crucial details to the heart-stricken family: 'Poor March was wounded very badly I much fear he will die…It will be sad that the best of so large a family shd die so young.'[15]

The letter contains a remarkable and rare remonstrance from Wellington against the senseless loss of life seen during these bloody battles, 'Day after day the best of his go down and no still no remorse. [There is] no check of conscience to those officials who are constantly calling out "War".'[16] He continues in a further letter 'March is declared out of all danger altho' the wound is very severe. I am delighted. I cannot well tell you how much I felt when I saw him extended on the field with all the marks of death upon him.'[17] The ball in March's chest was never removed, but despite this he was able to recover much of his former strength.

Orthez had been the final push in a long and bloody war and in April

1814 Napoleon finally abdicated. Finally, after over two decades of war in France, victory was declared and the British started to celebrate. William Pitt Lennox wrote:

> 'kings, emperors, princes, potentates, had flocked to London, which was thronged with the votaries of fashion and pleasure. Fêtes, operas, balls, masquerades, dinners, concerts, illuminations, naval and military reviews, formed the order of the day and night. Everybody was dining out, supping out, driving out, and hunting the royal and imperial lions.'[18]

In return for his services and sacrifices, Wellington was formally inaugurated in the House of Lords as a Baron, Viscount, Earl and Duke all at the same time; a unique ceremony not seen before or since. The name Wellington had been picked by his brother William after an area of Somerset where the family had originated before moving to Ireland in the fourteenth century. Henceforth the new Duke of Wellington became the most famous and beloved man in the country having saved Europe from the clutches of Napoleon.

On 30th May a peace settlement was drawn up between France and Britain, Russia, Austria and Prussia. The heads of these four super powers agreed to meet in London to discuss where the boundaries of a post-Napoleonic Europe would be marked. This was cause for an even grander celebration and that summer Goodwood played host to the Emperor of Russia and his sister the Grand Duchess of Oldenburgh. They expressed themselves 'highly delighted' with their stay. Meanwhile Wellington was made British Ambassador in Paris and was heartily welcomed as a bringer of peace by the people he had just liberated. That summer saw parties in Paris like never before and Wellington was greeted wherever he went with wholehearted thanks.

Meanwhile the Richmonds' financial worries had gone from bad to worse, not helped by the Duchess's gambling and shopping addiction. Relations between the couple had always been passionate but tempestuous. The Duchess was forced to endure her husband's affairs at close quarters and he in turn turned a blind eye to her frivolities, flirtations and financial excesses. Life in Ireland had certainly not been the cost effective plan they had hoped for. The extravagant lifestyle of entertaining that was expected of Richmond as Lord Lieutenant of Ireland had further increased the family debt by as much as £50,000.[19] March, now restored to heath, was twenty-five and little Sophia just five years old. Eleven other children remained and needed supporting including Georgy who was now a charming and vivacious seventeen year old, having grown confident in Phoenix Park's sheltered society.

The next few years would be the most exciting and character-forming years of Georgy's long life, for no one could have known that peace with France would only last a matter of months. The events that followed would mark one of the most significant battles in British history, and at the heart of that victory was Georgy's idol, the Duke of Wellington.

CHAPTER TWO

The Wash House

'The Duke of Wellington appears to unite those two extremes of character which Shakespeare gives to Henry the 5th: the hero, and the trifler.'[20]

Spencer Madan, tutor to the Lennox boys

In 1814 the Lennox family made plans to relocate again. The Duke of Richmond had been offered the position of Commander of the reserve forces stationed in Brussels. To his bitter disappointment he would be taking no active role in further military campaigns. Brussels had recently become an economical haven for those escaping debt and decadent living in England and was the prime destination for aristocratic, penniless families. They were attracted there by the large and comfortable houses available with cheap living costs. Running a large household and throwing regular events became feasible again for those society hostesses who had fallen on hard times. After the extravagances of life in Ireland it was an essential move for the Lennox family. Knowing that his friend John Capel was already settled in Brussels, Richmond wrote to him. Capel was married to Lady Caroline and they had a family that rivalled the Richmonds' in size. They too had relocated to Brussels to save money as Capel was a gambler with huge debts. Richmond wrote that he wanted to take his family to Brussels 'for a year on an Economical Plan,'[21] but Capel doubted if Richmond would be able to find a house large enough for his family. Brussels had become so popular that most of the good houses in the fashionable parts of town had already been taken.

The Capel family excitedly awaited the arrival of another family to join their social circle. Their daughter Lady Maria Capel wrote:

> 'Papa is quite delighted at the Prospect of seeing his old Friend again, & Ly Mary Lennox wrote a very kind letter to Harriet [Capel] the other day saying she looked forward with the greatest pleasure to our old Brighton Intimacy being renew'd. Lord March, who is here as one of the Pr. of O's ADC's, thinks they will not stay long. He is a very pleasant Person and has still a Ball in him from the Effects of which he has not recovered, but Faints at the least transition from heat to cold'.[2]

Lord March had recovered sufficiently from his injuries to become an A.D.C. to the highly bred but highly unreliable Prince of Orange, heir to the throne of the newly formed United Netherlands. The Prince had arrived in July 1814 but this had not caused as much interest amongst the British community stationed there as might have been expected. This was largely due to the fact that Princess Charlotte, only daughter of the Prince Regent, had broken off her engagement to the Prince on account of his publicly drunken behaviour. However, it was not long before 'Slender Billy' was winning friends with his enthusiasm for partying. He made it known that he intended to be 'very merry & to have Balls and Breakfasts without end,'[23] which endeared him to everybody of the same inclination.

Although the Prince was popular in the ballroom, no-one trusted him anywhere near a battlefield. When Georgy had settled into life in Brussels she saw a good deal of him and declared him to be 'inexperienced and rash.'[24] Georgy was far from star-struck when it came to the Prince, who could certainly never match up to Wellington. However, it appears that the Prince himself was rather taken with Georgy even if the feeling was not mutual. He gave her a present of a beautiful amber fan which she took, no doubt, to every ball to show off to her friends. The Prince of Orange and March became firm friends, seen constantly in each other's company. As heir to the Richmond ducal coronet, March was one of the most eligible young men on the Brussels social scene, as were his younger brothers Lieutenant George Lennox of the 9th Light Dragoons and William Pitt Lennox, who had had been A.D.C. to Wellington in Paris but was now to take the same position under General Sir Peregrine Maitland.

The picturesque town of Brussels was fast becoming the main outpost of London high society largely due to the presence of the Army who had had a base there since 1813. The town had held strong to Napoleon until the last throes of the Peninsular Campaign and there were still parts that remained loyal to him, hence the need for a military presence near the town. Despite this, no one considered that much military action was likely after Napoleon had been so soundly beaten by the Allies and exiled to the island of Elba in April 1814. The impact of the Army's presence in Brussels was mainly social. It provided a plethora of young men to invite to events and in their uniforms they added an extra frisson to the party atmosphere. The Army attracted a number of families to Brussels, especially those with daughters of a marriageable age. For Georgy, Brussels opened up a whole world of new social opportunities after the rather limited society in Dublin. Brussels was considered by much of the British aristocracy second only to London and Paris as the party capital of Europe.

With none of her elder sisters yet married Georgy needed to make herself stand out. At nineteen years of age, Georgy was considered a true English beauty and was arguably the most beautiful of all the Lennox daughters. She had a well-proportioned round face and clear pale complexion framed by curls of brown hair that were fashionable at the time. Her eyes were a dark chestnut brown, her dark features contrasting beautifully with her luminous and youthful skin. In character Georgy had certainly inherited some of her mother's sharp tongue but it was at least tempered by a good dose of her father's kind-hearted and generous nature.

The task of relocating the family was a long and arduous one, the logistics of which fell largely to the Duchess. The Duke of Richmond started the journey first with his two eldest daughters, Mary and Sarah, now aged twenty-three and twenty-two respectively. The Duchess was left behind to deal with moving the rest of the children. A tutor named Spencer Madan had recently joined the family to teach the younger boys and he was to accompany the Lennox family on their voyage to Brussels. His long, gossipy letters home are an invaluable source of information about the journey and the family. Spencer found the Duchess to be 'one of the sourest most illtempered personages I ever came across in my life' and found that each post she received brought 'some news that she does not like...One day she was angry because she did not receive a letter from the Duke, another because she did.'[25] The Duchess's volatile and high-handed behaviour does not appear to have affected her daughters. Spencer thought highly of them, writing that they were 'the most goodhumoured and unaffected girls I ever met with, exceedingly highbred but without an atom of pride. They do not deserve to be coupled with the Dss, whom they resemble but in name.'[26]

Travelling anywhere abroad in 1814 was long, arduous and uncomfortable. The party left Dublin on 28th September just after dawn, the Duchess making everyone late with her endless demands. The party travelled in two brand new carriages but the roads were in an appalling condition, dangerous for both horse and carriage. More hazardous were the gangs of vagrants and highwaymen preying on those who travelled the roads at night. The Duchess was not put off, intent as she was on re-joining her husband as fast as possible. Madan sends a report to his parents of their journey:

> 'We travelled in 2 new carriages exceedingly handsome & stylish. In the first were the Dss, Ladies Georgiana Jane Louisa & Charlotte, and her Grace's maid Mrs. Smith. There was only a boot before without a barouche box; in the rumble tumble sat Mr. Johnson the butler. Our carriage wch. was the barouche landau contained Lady Sophia & her maid my three pupils & self. on the barouche box Mr. Gillet a Brussels merchant whom the Dss carries over to pay her expenses in France, (he knows the coin and language of the country) and Mrs. Wood a ladies' maid.'[27]

The group of eighteen was crammed into two carriages because the Duchess refused to pay for another. The carriages were each pulled by six horses and completely packed with luggage (especially the second carriage, grumbled Spencer). This discomfort was met with a resigned acceptance by the nomadic Richmond clan who were by now used to regularly moving around in large numbers.

The party took two days to reach Dover. They set sail in a Royal Navy sloop, the HMS Redpole, led by Captain Denman who was attentive and put everyone at ease. A Naval salute was fired as the shipped pulled away from the shore around noon, a fitting tribute to the regal Duchess and her family. The family waved goodbye to England and by evening they had anchored off Boulogne in the pitch darkness. They were taken ashore by rowing boats but as the tide was out they were forced to walk a mile and a half through the wet and wild weather to the shore. The night was passed in a grotty and uncomfortable inn. Family and servants alike huddled together in the draughty rooms and attempted to get a few hours' sleep.

The journey from Boulogne to Calais was again rough and unpleasant. The children were not given enough food and so were grumpy and tired. At least at Calais they were greeted with a hearty dinner. Changing horses, the travelling party covered the next twenty-two miles to Dunkirk in good time. However, straightaway the Duchess expressed her desire to push on to Bruges. Every day of the journey was costing more money. She was also anxious that her husband had now been on his own for some time and she wanted to get to Brussels so she could keep a watchful eye over him. The Duke was known to indulge regularly in his favourite pastime of drinking gin and smoking until the early hours of the morning with any fellow who would sit up with him.[28] No doubt the Duchess wished to get to Brussels so that her husband did not have time to make too many close female friends in her absence.

In Brussels Mary and Sarah were not looking forward to the Duchess's arrival. They had already made a great number of friends and they could do without the interference of their mother. March was at this time ill and bedbound, perhaps related to his old war wound. He was in a 'precarious state,'[29] and hardly fit to cope with his overbearing mother either.

Despite the Duchess's insistence, no horses could be found to take them to Bruges. The entire group were forced to spend another freezing night sleeping in the two unprotected carriages. The next morning the party finally made it to the city and spent the day exploring. Bruges was described by John Capel's wife Caroline as 'the dirtiest dismal Place I ever saw, full of Prussians',[30] who were generally disliked by the British. However, for Georgy the gothic towers and turrets of the city were like nothing she had ever experienced before. From Bruges the carriages rumbled wearily on into Brussels itself.

It was Friday 14th October, on a grey and gloomy day nearly three weeks since they had left Dublin, when the family finally arrived in Brussels. Already the crispness of winter was drawing in. The carriages took them past the grand houses facing the park which had already been occupied by other leading expatriate families. The house in which the Lennoxes were to live was the only one the Duke had been able to procure. The rue de la Blanchisserie had been the site of a seventeenth- century laundry and was situated in the more industrial side of Brussels. The area was unkempt, with unpaved streets on which to drive the precious carriages. The area did not endear itself to the snobbish Duchess, who wanted one of the smarter houses in a better part of town, that she had seen from the carriage.

Yet the house that Richmond had secured for them was certainly grand enough. It was expansive with two large wings and a beautifully laid out garden. The house had been built thirty-five years previously by a coach-builder called Jean Simon. One side of the extensive garden bordered onto the ramparts with a view from the top of the house looking out over the city and the Palace of Lacken, home to the elder Prince of Orange. There was a separate house in the grounds for Lord March to keep his own residence. The right of the two wings, formerly the coachman's workshop, now served as an indoor play area and study room for the children. When the weather was inclement Georgy enjoyed playing games of battledore and shuttlecock there with her siblings. The younger boys ran wild in the garden, much to the chagrin of their tutor Spencer. The three youngest sisters, Louisa (known as Maria), eleven years, Charlotte, ten years, and little Sophia (known as Pen) five years, were looked after by a governess known only as 'Mademoiselle'. Georgy, Mary and Sarah were now chaperoned to events by their mother who made sure she kept a close eye on them. The Capels at least approved of the Richmonds' new house and as their children were of a similar age they were soon to be regular visitors to there:

> 'The Duke of Richmond [has] a delightfull [sic] House & Gardens in the Lower part of the Town, & delightful it ought to be, to at all compensate for the disadvantage of the situation.'[31]

The Duke had already settled into the pace of his new life. His position within the forces was mainly ceremonial and his work schedule not taxing. Although he was prone to moments of 'Gloomy Melancholy' he was universally loved for his warmth, kindness and sociability.[32] The Duchess too was surprised at how quickly she began to enjoy life in Brussels. After a few days of settling into the house, unpacking the multitude of cases and organising the children, the calendar of social events began and the Duchess entered society. There were so many 'Balls, Assemblies, and Parties of various descriptions…that not a single night passes without some engagement at home or abroad.' [33] The Duchess was the first to leave the house in the afternoon and the last to return at night. She always rose early despite only sleeping for three or four hours.[34] With so many social engagements and the prospect of so many eligible men for her daughters to meet, the Duchess struggled to find enough hours in the day.

Many of the large aristocratic families who had relocated to Brussels knew each other and socialised in a close-knit group. As well as the Capel family, the Richmonds were already acquainted with Sir Charles and Lady Charlotte Greville, who alongside Lady Caroline Capel and the Duchess of Richmond quickly became 'the principal English at Brussels.'[35] Called the 'Ladies in the Park', these society hostesses made it a rule only to visit those whom they had already known in London making it an oppressively elitist and limited social network.[36] These ladies may have presented a unified front of English high society but their true characters were gossiped about in whispers and in letters, such as this report about the Duchess of Richmond from Lady Georgiana Capel, Caroline Capel's daughter:

> 'We have seen a great deal of the Richmonds, the Duchess has taken very much to us but I do not think it will last as she is, you know, a difficult person to deal with and withal

> a dreadful mischief maker and is in constant correspondence with Lady Hertford [favourite of the Prince Regent] to whom she reports every word she hears of the Prince Regent, insomuch that the Lennoxs [sic] have warned us to be careful.'[37]

Brussels' three social mistresses threw event after event and Georgy was in attendance at many of them. Everyone was discussing the anticipated return of the great Duke of Wellington which was sure to send Brussels' social scene into overdrive.

Brussels was the perfect setting for an English family living abroad. Georgy and her family were thoroughly enjoying their new home. The park was considered to be one of the most beautiful in Europe and was a popular place for people to promenade together throughout the day. It was a formal rectangular shape surrounded by iron railings with gravel walkways, quite sophisticated for the time. The lawns were shaded by trees and interspersed with ornamental fountains and statues. At one side there was a small 'pleasure garden' called Vauxhall Gardens after its famous counterpart in south London. The entertainment programme in the park and in the theatres of the main town was varied and well-attended by both the British and Belgian communities. The Windsor theatrical company performed there with the celebrated Mrs Jordan, who had been so embarrassed by the Duke of Richmond's proposal several years earlier. During the day the troops trained in the park and their officers provided a constant stream of eligible men to invite to the never-ending calendar of balls, dinners, picnics, theatre trips, races, hunts, military reviews and shopping trips. Indeed, war was a distant memory to most of the expatriate community in Brussels.

For the first time in Georgy's life her family no longer needed to fret over their expensive lifestyle, which was a most exciting prospect for a young lady who enjoyed clothes and fine things. The prices in Brussels meant that a flat-broke aristocratic family could enjoy the luxuries and excesses of the life expected of their class without cascading into further debt. The ludicrous exchange rate and the varied supply of commercial goods on offer delighted everyone. Spencer commented 'Things are certainly cheap as dirt here.'[38] Harriet Capel delighted in 'how cheap everything is here and the exchange is improving every day.'[39] The Duchess no longer feigned guilt at her extravagant spending and Georgy and her sisters could go shopping on the Grande Place whenever they pleased. They often went with the Capels, buying 'the most beautiful silk & Satin shoes here for 4s 6d a pair and & walking shoes for 3s 6d- Gloves, Silks, Ribbons, as cheap',[40] as well as 'the best long white gloves 2s 6d per pair- 4 pair of satin shoes for 18 shillings, thick sarsnet for gowns, the most beautiful colours.'[41] These beautiful cloths were made into new clothes and worn out at the earliest opportunity.

Popular events included regular race meetings which became a favourite of the Richmond set: 'We have had some very Gay races recently, the Young Prince, Duke of Richmond & many others have Horses run & many of the Gentlemen ride themselves- They rather astonish the Natives.'[42] Both officers and civilians, including March and his father, brought over their racehorses from England. Many of the participants were Guards and Cavalry Officers letting off steam and displaying their skill in the saddle in front of families and friends who gathered to watch. Reports of these races appeared in the English newspapers and became known as the 'Brussels Races'.

2. Cariacture of the 1st Duke of Wellington telling off Georgy's brother William Pitt Lennox, a sketch for his published reminiscences of life as a Lennox.
© Tate Britain, London

More amateur races were often organised by the young officers as challenges to each other. William Pitt Lennox, now fifteen years old, was a rather wild and unruly youth. One day he was visiting the picturesque village of Enghein, well known by the British for its beautiful lake and popular cricket ground. William agreed to a race from a fellow officer, mounted his Cossack steed and set off at a roaring speed around the lake. The horse bolted into a wood, throwing William off and smashing him into a tree. The accident left him lying unconscious for seventy-two hours in General Maitland's headquarters, when it seemed as though he might not survive. The incident took place after Wellington had at last arrived in Brussels and, sensing hysterics from the Duchess, he waited until the initial danger had passed before he wrote to Sarah Lennox: 'It is true that William has had a fall from his horse, which appeared yesterday rather a serious one. I am waiting for March to go down to the Duchess to let her know it, and you had better say nothing about it till I shall arrive.'[43] Reckless William's injuries proved serious enough to keep him on the sick list and off the battlefield that was soon to come.

Hunting was another popular past time, but as it led to party-goers being absent for up to two weeks at a time, it was not so popular with their dancing partners. The Capels moaned:

> 'a Grand Wolf Hunting to take place in the Forest of Ardennes about 50 Miles from here. It is to last a fortnight – Papa & the Duke of Richmond are Prime Movers &, as it carries them & The Cream of our Society off, we think it a great Bore.' [44]

When not out racing or hunting, many convened on the Richmond house which had become the gossip hub of Brussels life. Visitors with news were always welcome with or without an invitation. Mary, Sarah and Georgy were all now old enough to begin enjoying Brussels as young woman ready for romance. They were certainly spoilt for choice with the majority of officers coming from upper class or aristocratic families. The Duchess was thrilled with the attention the sisters were receiving but as Spencer records in one of his letters, she formally warned her daughters not to associate themselves romantically with anyone below the rank of an Earl.[45] Dancing or talking in an overly-familiar fashion with such men was strictly monitored although the Duchess quickly found that this was difficult to enforce. Richmond also tried to ban his daughters from partaking in the Waltz, the newly fashionable dance where partners held each other close across the dancefloor, as he deemed it too racy. The Lennox sisters defied both their parents from the outset, they flirted and waltzed with whoever the pleased. Their dance cards were always full and they always delighted their dinner-table companions, whether aristocratic or not.

However, Georgy had no trouble meeting men who did fit her mother's requirements. Her title, social polish and close friendship with Wellington made her a magnet for male attention and their tight-knit social group had from the outset squeezed out most unsuitable dance partners. It was not long before the Duchess had set her sights on a possible match for Georgy in the form of Lord Beaumont Hotham who had recently succeeded his grandfather to become the 3rd Baron Hotham. She insisted on taking them both to the Hague to give them time to get to know each other and at parties ensured they were always in each other's company.[46] Georgiana Capel wrote that Captain Hotham was: 'quite young, in the Guards, hideously ugly, very stingy and has £20,000 a year.'[47] which was low praise indeed, and may go some way to explain why the romance got off to such a bumpy start. No doubt it was Hotham's fortune that had attracted the Duchess to him but Georgy needed much more convincing. The Earl of Malmsbury wrote:

> 'Brussels is a perfect manufactory of matches. Amongst others which are in progress is one between a particular friend of mine, Lord Hotham, and Lady Georgiana Lennox (the third daughter); this is, however, a profound secret at present, though of course known to about half the world. You must not, therefore, quote me. The lady is as near perfection as human nature admits of, and in every respect the most delightful girl I ever saw.'[48]

Georgy was young and had little experience of courting and romance but she knew that she did not return Hotham's passions as her mother wished. She knew her own mind and would not be pushed into a marriage she feared she would later regret. Although she continued to see Hotham socially, his visits were soon surpassed by visits from Wellington after his arrival in April. Georgy and the Duke loved to gossip about the men that befriended the Lennox sisters and they nicknamed Hotham 'The Enemy'. The Duke did not think him an appropriate match for his 'Dearest Georgy',as he called her in letters. The Duchess continued to push for an agreement between Georgy and Hotham but was partially distracted by the love affairs of Georgy's sister Sarah, who had been conducting a romance with both Lord O'Neil and Lord Apsley at the same time; although neither came to fruition.[49] Sarah, like all the Lennox sisters, needed to marry money and neither of these suitors boasted enough of a fortune to satisfy the exacting standards of the Duchess of Richmond.

Despite 'The Enemy' pursuing Georgy at every opportunity, our heroine had already set her sights on another man in the form of the dashing Sir Felton Hervey-Bathurst. Of all of Wellington's staff, Felton was the Duke's absolute favourite having shared with him many adventures over the plains of the Iberian Peninsula. It was during one of these adventures that heroic Felton had had an arm amputated which naturally led to an increase in admiration from his female friends. Although Georgy and the Duke delighted in discussing her current conquests of the heart, on this occasion she did not confide in him her feelings for Felton. It is not until over a year later that Wellington wrote to her from Paris: 'You are a little Witch! You never told me that you had bewitched my Secretary [Hervey Bathurst]! He is going about very poorly [love-sick]!"[50] It appears though that whatever had existed between the pair did not last because only a few months after Wellington found out about her affection for Felton, the dashing young suitor had married another woman. Wellington wrote again from Paris:

> 'I propose to go over [to London] for the Regents birthday & Col. Herveys Marriage which will have surprised you not a little. I hope you make a better impression in other quarters; but although he was certainly poorly when I returned from England last Christmas, he appears to have recovered as soon as it was possible.'[51]

This was Georgy's first foray into the adult world of love and courting and she had been left unsatisfied. She had been cast aside for the popular American heiress Louisa Caton whose sister Marianne Paterson was to make a great impression on the Duke of Wellington. Georgy would go on to treat Louisa rather cruelly, showing a glint of her mother's coldness.

~

The year 1815 was brought in with snow and freezing cold. But the houses were well lit with wax candles and hearths heartened with roaring fires. Balls were scheduled nearly every week at each of the big houses in turn. The parties lasted longer and were better attended than ever before as even more expatriate families had joined the fun. Yet peace was not to last. Wellington was currently away representing Britain at the Congress of Vienna, whose task it was to decide how best to split European power after the decimation of Napoleon's empire the previous year. Meanwhile Napoleon, exiled on the island of Elba, was quickly recovering his political strength and had begun to plot his escape. As audacious and brave as Wellington, Napoleon still commanded huge respect and loyalty from his French troops, who were as desperate as their master to reclaim their fallen empire. During the Congress of Vienna, news reached the plenipotentiaries there that Napoleon had escaped with a contingent of loyal soldiers and was gathering an army around him. War was declared within an hour of news reaching Vienna. Napoleon had wasted no time, he had marched into Paris and taken control of the government without a single shot being fired. Louis XVIII had fled with his crown and his jewels, leaving his dignity behind. Soon Napoleon left Paris, and he began the march in the direction of Brussels to reclaim his empire on the battlefield against Wellington and his Allied armies.

Such news sent shockwaves through the community in Brussels who were now vulnerable and in the line of fire for a direct attack from Napoleon. From the beginning of March the inhabitants of Brussels had known that Napoleon was leading his army their way. The atmosphere changed and there was tension in the air as each morning brought war closer. Daily exchanges became increasingly charged as rumours flew from mouth and letter all around town. Families began to make plans to leave and many more sent away their belongings for safe keeping. Lady de Lancey was one of the many women who were sent to Antwerp to await the fate of their husbands. She had become well known in Brussels for her beauty and for her marriage to Wellington's popular Quarter-Master General Sir William de Lancey. They had only been married two months, yet her story would soon be a tragic one.

In Brussels everyone was desperate for Wellington to return from Vienna and ready the Allied army to face Napoleon. Georgy recalled:

> 'there was great anxiety among the English officers for the Duke's arrival, as the Prince of Orange would otherwise have been in command. The Prince was quite angry with me for sharing this feeling, exclaiming, "Why have you no confidence in me?", to which I replied "Well, sir, you have not been tried and the Duke has".'[52]

This response did not go down well. Wellington had immediately made plans to leave the Congress of Vienna as soon as he heard the news of Napoleon's escape. After a long and arduous journey he and his entourage arrived in Brussels late in the evening of 4th April. The rumours of his imminent arrival had reached boiling point and bubbled over as he rode into the city. Families and militia alike flocked to line the streets and shouts of joy and encouragement rang out. Finally, their hero had arrived. Wellington returned to his large house on the rue de la Montagne du Parc, but did not rest after his journey, throwing himself into the administration of war. It would take all his renowned organisational skills to put back together an army which had been disbanded only the previous year.

Soon after the Duke's arrival, the rather overshadowed Prince of Orange officially resigned his command of the Army. This left Wellington in sole charge of all the Allied forces as their Field Marshal. Yet this was not the old battle-hardened army which he had commanded in the Peninsular War, as many of the skilled veterans of this campaign had since retired or died. Wellington exclaimed: 'I have got an infamous army, very weak and ill equipped and a very inexperienced staff.'[53] The men themselves were largely recent recruits, untested in battle, ill-disciplined and unpredictable. Wellington did not feel he could trust them. Having watched them at their worst during the looting frenzies of the Peninsular War, he had famously condemned them as the 'scum of the earth.'[54] Would they prove more reliable this time round?

If Wellington despaired, it was in private only. In public he put on a front of calm efficiency and, despite his gruelling work schedule, began to party again with gusto. Georgy was delighted to be reunited with him and they saw each other regularly. Wellington was also returned to his drinking companion and old friend Richmond and became a regular presence on the Rue de La Blanchisserie which he fondly called 'The Wash House'. Wellington continued to entertain enthusiastically:

> 'No one would suppose hostilities will soon commence judging by the Duke of Wellington. He gives a ball every week, attends every party, partakes of every amusement that offers. Yesterday he took Lady Jane Lennox to Enghein for the cricket match and bought her back at night apparently having gone for no other object but to amuse her. At the time Bonaparte was said to be at Mauberge, 30 or 40 miles off'.[55]

The Richmonds relaxed their rules with regards to chaperoning when it came to Wellington, who was allowed to socialise with each of the Lennox sisters in turn. His honour was not to be called into question. On 22nd May it was Georgy's turn and she accompanied the Duke on a review of the Duke of Brunswick's regiment. It was often the habit of Wellington to take his young female friends on these impressive official visits. It was the perfect opportunity to show off his own position of power and authority within the Army whilst enjoying a day out with a friend. It was a cold and wet day when they set out for the review, riding across the grassy plains. Row upon row of troops stood to attention like painted toy soldiers. Georgy's pride at accompanying Wellington must have been great. After the review, as the weather worsened, Lord Uxbridge found a soldier's great-coat to wrap around Georgy for the trip home. Uxbridge was a military man of great renown who had recently been lying low due to his affair with Lady Charlotte Wellesley, the 1st Duke's sister-in-law. Uxbridge and Lady Charlotte had recently divorced their respective partners and married each other, a scandal practically unheard of at the time. However, soon the battle would bring Wellington and Uxbridge together in a way neither could have imagined.

During this period the correspondence between Georgy and Wellington demonstrates a heightened level of intimacy. The Duke was still a virile and fun-loving man who enjoyed the company of the beautiful women who flocked around him. No doubt Georgy was totally besotted with the Duke. There is no evidence to suggest that their relationship went beyond a strong flirtation, and every woman who was friends with Wellington throughout his life would have to endure jealous rumours from others that their relationship had gone further. Wellington was married and was already conducting a number of affairs during his limited free time. These were known about publicly but discussed in whispers and in any case Wellington always acted with the height of discretion. He was often accompanied at parties by either the beautiful Lady Charlotte Greville or the wild Lady Frances Wedderburn-Webster, both of whom he was conducting affairs with. This behaviour was not unusual in the heated atmosphere of pre-battle Brussels, however scandal was discouraged. On the surface no hint was given of the true extent of Wellington's relationship with these women. Caroline Capel wrote 'The Duke of W- has not improved the Morality of our Society as he has given several things [balls] & makes a point of asking all the Ladies of Loose Character.'[56]

Lady Charlotte Greville, known by most as the Duke's First Lady, revelled in her intimacy with him during this period. Yet she did have to share his affections with the beautiful and highly strung Frances Wedderburn-Webster. Frances was already well known due to the rumoured affair she had had with her husband's close friend, Lord Byron. The Duke's affair with her quickly became notorious and was mentioned in papers both in Brussels and in London. One staff officer recalled seeing Wellington in the park in Brussels when 'a carriage drove up and a lady got out of it and joined him. They went down into a hollow where the trees completely screened them.'[57] This was Frances and after a moment her mother, Lady Mountnorris, also turned up 'searching in vain for her daughter.'[58] Luckily for the lovers, trees successfully hid them from view. What is even more surprising is that Frances was seven months pregnant at the time. Frances's husband was also a notorious adulterer but he now decided to sue one newspaper for printing details of the affair between his wife and the Duke of Wellington. For this the Wedderburn-Websters were awarded damages to the tune of £2,000; a very large sum for the time. Later on, after the affair with Wellington had ended, Frances continued to receive a pension from him until her death in 1837. That Wellington could juggle a full social calendar, countless female admirers and the orchestration of one of the most complex military manoeuvres of the nineteenth century was extraordinary. Wellington was playing multiple parts on the stage set in Brussels in the months preceding Waterloo. We will never know for sure how Georgy felt about her beloved hero's scandalous pre-Waterloo affairs. Whatever her feelings in private, they remained close.

Rumours of the imminent invasion continued and an awareness of the proximity of war soon began to affect life in Brussels. Wellington did not reveal openly any anxiety he had for those who chose to remain in Brussels nor about the poor state of the different armies he commanded. Yet there were rare occasions when this façade slipped. Georgy asked him whether a party planned by some officers could take place close to the border at Tournay or Lille. The Duke's immediate response was: "No; better let that drop", he knew the border was now too dangerous, swarming as it was with Napoleonic troops.[59] Georgy did not press the matter. Luckily for the Lennox sisters the balls did not stop. Caroline Capel wrote in June: 'Balls are going on here as if we had had none for a year'.[60] Wellington held one himself on 3rd June, and attended one the next night at the British Embassy. Two nights later he held another. Caroline Capel continued:

> '...Nobody can guess the Lord Wellington's intentions & I dare say Nobody will know he is going till he is actually gone. In the meantime he amuses himself with Humbugging the Ladies, particularly the Duchess of Richmond.'[61]

The rumours were so constant and changeable that people began to disregard them. Georgy herself placed no importance on the stories she heard even when the rumour mill began again in the days leading up to 15th June. In any case she was too busy preparing for an event scheduled to take place that evening. It was to be the Richmonds' turn to host a ball and the whole family was involved in the preparations. Georgy would have been eagerly planning her outfit and thinking of the officers she would dance with. She had no idea that her mother's ball would go down in history as the society event which heralded the start of the most dramatic battle in British history.

CHAPTER THREE

The Ball

'The history of a battle, is not unlike the history of a ball. Some individuals may recollect all the little events of which the great result is the battle won or lost, but no individual can recollect the order in which, or the exact moment at which, they occurred, which makes all the difference as to their value or importance...'[62]

The 1st Duke of Wellington

At the Duchess's ball the gilded bubble of peacetime partying was broken. The event has since become known as a marker of those few precious hours between peace and war. Guests enjoyed the frivolities and luxuries of a society event before enduring the horror of waving goodbye to men who would not return to dance another day. That night Napoleon and his troops invaded the Kingdom of the Netherlands and made a slow but determined advance towards Brussels. The nostalgic and often romanticised reminiscences of those who attended the Duchess of Richmond's ball have weaved myth and fantasy into the evening's proceedings. Many attendees, Georgy included, felt a huge sense of pride in having been there on that fateful evening. Georgy's presence at the ball and her connection with Wellington at this time would colour the rest of her life. What she witnessed of the man she hero-worshipped would only add to her passionate feelings for him. It was with awe and a growing sense of personal pride that she watched the drama unfold that evening.

The Lennoxes tutor Spencer wrote two days before the ball:

> 'Tho' I have given some pretty good reasons for supposing that hostilities will soon commence, yet no one wd. Suppose it judging by the Duke of Wn. He appears to be thinking of anything else in the world, gives a ball every week, attends every party and partakes of every amusement that offers.'[63]

Throwing a ball when war was so close at hand was indeed a risky business so the Duchess sought the advice of Wellington before organising her own: 'I do not wish to pry into your secrets, nor do I ask what your intentions may be, I wish to give a ball, and all I ask, is may I give a ball? If you say, "Duchess, don't give a ball," it is quite sufficient,' she said, adding magnanimously 'I ask no reasons.'[64] Wellington replied: 'Duchess, you may give your ball with the greatest safety, without fear of interruption',[65] and so preparations began in earnest. Wellington himself intended to throw a ball on 21st June, the anniversary of the Battle of Vitoria. The timing for the Duchess's ball was perfect. Had Napoleon decided to invade a day earlier, then the famous event would instead have been called 'Lady Conyngham's Ball', for this equally lavish party had been thrown the evening of 14th

June. The Duchess's luck was in, although perhaps she would not have agreed as she was less than impressed when the majority of her guests abandoned her carefully prepared evening for the battlefield.

Although the event is often remembered as a formal 'farewell' to soldiers leaving for the front, it was in fact a private party organised by the Duchess of Richmond. She was free to invite whomever she pleased. A practiced hostess with the perfect opportunity to present her young and beautiful daughters to society, she rose graciously to the challenge. Even under the strained circumstances of organising a ball amid a mobilising army, she orchestrated a particularly lavish and glittering event. An invitation to the ball was a golden ticket and it was the event on everybody's lips. There was a good mix of people invited, Belgian and Dutch, French, German, and of course a plethora of socially well-connected and aristocratic English. In total 228 invitations were issued although it is likely that around 200 people attended including ten members of the Richmond family.[66] Several of the officers invited were not present as they were on duty. Of those who did attend, one third were serving officers and despite their lack of titles many of them were seen by the Duchess as eligible dance partners for her daughters. The Duke had been forced to abandon his ban on the Waltz which would feature heavily in the evening's proceedings.

The exact location of the ball was disputed long after the event but Georgy and her siblings, William and Louisa, all later confirmed that it was held in the old coach-builder's workshop situated to the left of the main house and connected to it by an annex.[67] The room had two floors with the upper level providing a convenient setting where guests dined mid-way through the evening. The main dancehall had been papered with a rose trellis pattern before the arrival of the Richmond family. The image of that room, with its low ceiling and shimmering candlelight, would remain one of Georgy's most vivid memories throughout her life. The tale of the night became a favourite one to retell in later years when the romance of the night's events had somewhat overtaken the facts.

On the day itself, the Lennox residence teemed with servants who had been lent to them for the evening by the British Ambassador. The fine dinner service had also been sent over from the British Embassy.[68] In the house servants brought in tables and chairs, polished glasses and arranged the position of the band which had been provided by the Army. The Duchess was on the war path ensuring that every task was completed to her satisfaction, every place set perfect, every glass polished. Her daughters were grateful to escape and relax in the house's formal gardens that afternoon. The excitement of having such a grand ball at their own house was thrilling to the Lennox girls and they would have given little thought to the ominous rumours spreading from house to house about Napoleon's advance. This carefree feeling was reinforced after a visit from Lord Arthur Hill who was one of Wellington's A.D.C.s. Lord Hill flatly denied any rumours of an imminent invasion.[69] Instead the happy group discussed the details of the evening's activities, their dresses, the men they would see and which of the sisters would fill their dance cards first.

There was a very different feeling prevailing amongst the military. It was clear that action was about to commence. From the morning of 15th June Wellington received information that the French were advancing but this intelligence was not sufficiently worrying for him to command any mass movement of troops. He continued in a calm and efficient manner, perhaps barking his orders a little sharper as he sent his A.D.C.s flying across town with orders and messages. He was to hold his own pre-ball dinner later that evening where the Prince of Orange was to be guest of honour. At around 5pm Wellington was walking in the shade of the park, giving orders and receiving the latest intelligence from his staff officers. He still intended to go to the Duchess's ball and passed the word around that he expected as many officers as possible to attend. In this way Wellington would have all his A.D.C.s and officers in one place, ready to receive instructions. It was also most unlike the Duke to miss a chance for a party with his closest friends. By late afternoon, when Georgy was starting to get ready, gunfire could be heard just south of Brussels.

As the Allies readied themselves for battle, the party goers prepared themselves for the evening's event. Georgy and her sisters changed into their pale satin gowns with wide silk ribbons around their waists. The sky fell into a clear bright night and it was time for the ball to begin. No expense had been spared in the preparation of the ballroom or the Lennox girls' outfits. The guests began arriving at around 10pm, greeted by the Duke and Duchess with their children in attendance. Everyone was dressed in their finest attire with sparkling diamonds and military medals glinting in the candlelight. The pale satin of the ladies' dresses was offset by the scarlet of the officers' uniforms: Guardsmen, Hussars and infantryman alike. The Prince of Orange was in his customary scarlet uniform of a British General and the Duke of Brunswick in his uniform of jet black. Wellington was notable by his absence. He was still in his own quarters, engaged in some rapid letter writing and discussing last minute details with de Lancey and Fitzroy Somerset, two of his most trusted aides. Events were moving quickly and Wellington knew that a clash with the French was imminent.

Wellington finally arrived at the ballroom at around midnight accompanied by Baron von Müffling, the Prussian liaison officer. William Pitt Lennox recalled that Wellington 'entered the ball-room, paid his respects to my mother with his customary high-bred courtesy, and continued to chat playfully to my sisters, not forgetting a kind pressure on the hand to myself.'[70] Georgy was already dancing when Wellington entered the ballroom but immediately abandoned her dance partner to go to him. She later recounted:

> '[I] at once went up to ask him about the rumours. He said very gravely, "Yes, they are true; we are off tomorrow." This terrible news was circulated directly, and while some of the officers hurried away, others remained at the ball, and actually had not time to change their clothes, but fought in evening costume.'[71]

She continued, 'It was a dreadful evening, taking leave of friends and acquaintances, many never to be seen again. The Duke of Brunswick, as he took leave of me in the ante-room adjoining the ball-room, made me a civil speech as to the Brunswickers being sure to distinguish themselves after 'the honour' done them by me having accompanied the Duke of Wellington to their Review!'[72] Georgy was much impressed with this speech but little did she know that this was to be the last time she would see the friendly Duke, whose troops she had so recently admired whilst attending the Review with Wellington.

For those that remained, supper was served and Georgy had the privilege of sitting next to Wellington at dinner. It must have been a proud and memorable moment for Georgy to be given this prime position next to the Duke and a true honour considering the occasion. What they discussed is not known, nor is how Georgy felt at this moment, as she never recorded the conversation. We do know however that it was now that the Duke chose to give Georgy a memento for her to remember him by: a most valuable miniature of himself by the renowned Belgian artist Simon-Jacques Rochard. It was a poignant moment and undoubtedly this was a truly intimate gesture which, it could be argued, went beyond that of friendship. The uniqueness of this miniature, afterwards copied several times, is that it has preserved Wellington's likeness just before the battle which confirmed him as one of the greatest military heroes in British history. Georgy guarded this precious gift for the rest of the evening and it became an object of much jealousy to her sisters and friends.

As dinner drew to a close, Lieutenant Harry Webster, one of the Prince of Orange's A.D.C.s, arrived having galloped full-pelt through the night. He brought with him a letter containing the shocking news that the French were much closer than expected and were headed their way. There was a moment however, with Webster lingering in the doorway splattered in mud after his ride, that time stood still. Webster watched and waited, as polite society dictated, whilst the company rose from dinner. Georgy's mother was accompanied by the Prince of Orange and Wellington escorted Charlotte Greville and the rest of the group to the ballroom to continue dancing. Webster hastened to the Prince of Orange and handed him the despatch, who handed it straight to Wellington unopened, who placed it in his pocket and continued downstairs with Lady Charlotte. Only once this social protocol had been completed could Wellington slip away to read the note. He then returned and informed Webster to make ready the Prince of Orange's carriage to return its owner to headquarters at Braine-le-Comte. In that moment, he announced the battle had begun. The Duke remained calm and composed as he issued commands to the men who now crowded around him.

After they had received their orders, the men began to bid their farewells to friends and family, dashing from the ballroom and into the night. The music faltered as men began to depart. For the women suddenly stranded it was a bewildering and sobering moment. Jane Lennox recalled:

> 'Well I remember the rising from that supper-table, and all that followed immediately after it. I know I was in a state of wild delight; the scene itself was so stirring, and the company so brilliant, I recollect, on reaching the ballroom after supper, I was scanning over my tablets [dance-card], which were filled from top to bottom with the names of the partners to whom I was engaged; when, on raising my eyes, I became aware of a great preponderance of ladies in the room. White muslins and tarlatans abounded; but the gallant uniforms had sensibly diminished.'[73]

The sorrowful image of Jane standing neglected on the edge of the dance floor was one shared by many other ladies that evening. Although she was not in attendance at the ball, a letter sent by Caroline Capel summed the drama up well:

> 'In the midst of the dancing an express arrived to the Duke with an account of the Prussians having been beat and the French having advanced within 14 miles of Bruxelles- You may imagine the Electrical Shocks of such intelligence- Most of the Women in Floods of tears and all the Military in an instant collected round their respective leaders and in less than

20 minutes the room was cleared.'[74]

'Electric shocks' is a particularly effective way of describing the reaction to the news. Men abandoned the party in droves whilst women wept and implored them to stay. Small knots of friends crammed into doorways shouting out to others who passed. Lord Uxbridge called out to the general crowd 'You gentlemen who have engaged partners, had better finish your dance, and get to your quarters as soon as you can.'[75]

During the course of the evening Georgy left for a short time to help March pack in his residence. As an A.D.C., it was unlikely that March would get close enough to the main action to be in any real danger but naturally Georgy was still very worried for his safety. March was wildly excited, as were many of the young men, at the opportunity to prove themselves on the battlefield. Before she knew it he had dashed away through the crowds to join the Prince of Orange, leaving Georgy to return to the main ballroom.

Back at the ball and amongst the chaos, the Gordon Highlanders decided to go ahead with a display of their national dancing, alongside pipers, which had been organised by the Duchess. Her father the Duke of Gordon had raised the Highlanders regiment in 1794. Louisa Lennox recalled the moment:

> 'I well remember the Gordon Highlanders dancing reels at the ball; my mother thought it would interest the foreigners to see them, which it did. I remember hearing that some of the poor men who danced in our house were killed at Waterloo.'[76]

Whether they had an avid audience at this point is unlikely and it adds a particularly bizarre element to the evening's chaotic proceedings with Scottish Highlanders dancing and playing, but no-one paying them any attention.

Meanwhile Wellington had taken Richmond to one side to ask whether he had a map of the local area to hand. The two men disappeared to Richmond's study, where, in the company of one of his closest friends, Wellington burst out: 'Napoleon has humbugged me by God, he has gained twenty-four hours march on me.'[77] Richmond asked Wellington what he would do and he replied that the Allied Army would concentrate at Quatre-Bras, 'but we shall not stop him there, and, if so, I must fight him here' and he placed him thumb on the small village of Waterloo.[78] The spot was marked on the map with pencil, after which he wished Richmond 'adieu' and exited through a side door.[79] Wellington left the ball directly and as no account records anyone taking their farewell of him after this point, it is likely that he left without saying goodbye to any of his friends.

The Duchess remained at the entrance to the house imploring those leaving to stay a little while longer so as not to spoil the party. Many people were desperately trying to locate loved ones and perhaps snatch a quick kiss in parting. When Georgy returned from March's house she saw some 'energetic and heartless young ladies still dancing', despite the chaos around them. She later heard it said that 'the Ladies Lennox…did not do the honours of the ball well,'[80] implying that they had been the ones still dancing, but this was not the case. Instead Georgy walked around the ballroom comforting several ladies with tear-stained cheeks who were upset by the sudden departure of their beaus. As Georgy left she encountered Lord Hay, the 'dashing, merry youth, full of military ardour, whom I knew very well'; he was a close friend of William Lennox's. She was quite 'provoked' by him 'for his delight at going into action; and of all the honours he was to gain.'[81] For so many of the greener officers the next few days meant adventure and a chance to prove themselves but to the women they left behind there was only the fear of death and injury to those that they loved.

Such was the speed of Napoleon's approach towards Brussels that the Lennox sisters were left to an empty house within an hour of Webster's dispatch. They spent a restless night analysing the evening and worrying about what would happen over the next few days. Others questioned why Wellington did not act sooner: 'This has indeed come upon us like a Thief in the Night- I am afraid our Great Hero must have been deceived for he has certainly been taken by surprise.'[82] Eventually Georgy returned to her room, gazing at the precious miniature of Wellington he had given her. Treasuring this work as she would for the rest of her life, Georgy retained her faith in the Duke and prayed for the safety of her friends and family preparing to take to the battlefield.

What is fascinating about the ball is how quickly it was over. Weeks of preparation resulted in only a few hours of dining and dancing, interrupted by the arrival of Webster's news. The ball is now famous for heralding in the Battle of Waterloo which took place over the next three days. The evening had been one of the most exciting of Georgy's life but now she would witness the horrors of war through those she saw returned from the battlefield. The battle itself would become more famous than either Georgy or the Duke of Wellington could have ever imagined.

CHAPTER FOUR

Witnessing Waterloo

The loss is quite dreadful, but never was there so complete a victory'[82a]

Lady Sarah Lennox to Lady Georgina Bathurst
19th June 1815

As Caroline Capel wrote: 'To the English Ear unaccustomed to such things, the Cannonading of a Real Battle is Awful beyond description and to have one's friends walk out of one's Drawing Room into Action, which has literally been the case on this occasion, is a sensation far beyond description.'[83] The women left behind could do nothing but wait for news and pray that their loved ones would be spared. The mental tortures felt by mothers and sisters alike must have been very great. Georgy herself could not sleep and paced around the house listening to the crashes and shouts in the street below, the sounds of an army on the move. After a restless night the sun rose on infantry regiments preparing to march in the Place Royale. It was to become a clear bright day, tension hanging in the cold air. Lady De Lancey, married to Wellington's Quarter-Master General, recalled the solemn melancholy of the scene: 'Fifes played alone, and the regiments one after the other marched past, and I saw them melt away through the great gate at the end of the Square. Shall I ever forget the tunes played by the shrill fifes and the buglehorns which disturbed the night!'[84] Another observer wrote: 'The army were gone, and Brussels seemed a perfect desert. The mourners they had left behind were shut up in their solitary chambers, and the faces of the few who were slowly wandering about the streets were marked with deepest anxiety and melancholy.'[85]

Georgy too watched the men march towards the battlefield knowing that many would not return. That morning she wrote to her aunt Lady Bathurst:

> 'The Army is alas! ordered to march. The Guards were to leaven Enghien at five this morning, it was supposed they would only go to Braine le Comte. We had a great ball last night, and fancy seeing the horror of hearing this news in the middle of it, and of seeing all one's friends fly to the right and to the left. Dear little Tim [the Hon. Seymour Bathurst] was with us and my darling March, Tim was quite well, and they all either were in high spirits or affected to be so. The Duke expected to be obliged to go to-day. George [Lennox] went out early this morning to him, and is not yet returned, nor have we heard from him, so they are not gone. We are to be prepared to move if it is necessary, but I trust it will not be so.'[86]

There are many extensive accounts of the days that followed which would later be known as the Battle of Waterloo. Those fascinated by the extraordinary circumstances of this meeting of Wellington's Allied forces against Napoleon's can turn to Lady Longford's well-thumbed account or more recent books written by Rory Muir or Bernard Cornwall. This book does not seek to recount each dispatch and military manoeuvre which were of course unknown to Georgy and only recorded in full much later. Needless to say the facts stand thus: Wellington took to the battlefield facing the might of Napoleon's army. The Emperor's forces were never stronger or fiercer, buoyed by the presence of their revered leader. Early in the morning of 16th June the Duke set out from Brussels with his A.D.C.s and entered the battlefield at Quatre Bras. He cut a fine figure in his simple uniform of blue coat and dark hat, riding his favourite chestnut charger Copenhagen. He rode out in high spirits, and his A.D.C.s were proud to ride alongside him. Finally, after weeks of anticipation the army was on the move.

At Quatre Bras the Dutch-Belgian troops led by the Prince of Orange were outnumbered three to one. From a nearby windmill Wellington and Blücher were met with a sobering sight. The short but proud figure of Bonaparte himself could be seen through Wellington's telescope, along with the might of the French army. It was the first time Wellington had ever seen him and the closest the two would ever come to each other. It was clear to the Duke that the Prussian troops were in a terribly exposed position but Blücher refused to move them. By the end of the first act the Allies had suffered heavy losses and Blücher's army had been forced into a humiliating retreat to the east. Wellington was left with no choice but to follow suit. It was crucial that the French did not drive a wedge between the two forces. Wellington trusted that Blücher would return in time to swell the Allies numbers when he would need them most. The Forest of Soignes provided good cover and the ridge near the little known village of Waterloo was nearby. Wellington knew the ground well. This would be the place to stand and fight Napoleon.

As the battle progressed over the next day news began to filter back to Brussels about the vast numbers of casualties on the ground. Several of the staff officers known to Georgy and her sisters were killed or injured during these days. Two of the first deaths to be reported were Lord Hay and the Duke of Brunswick. Lord Hay had been a close friend of William Pitt Lennox's, in whose opinion there was never 'a finer fellow.'[87] Hay was killed riding his fine horse Abelard, dressed in such splendid attire that it was said that he was targeted because he dressed and acted like a senior officer. Less than twelve hours previously he had spoken to Georgy at the ball. The Duke of Brunswick, who had also spoken to Georgy at the ball about the honour that his regiment would do, could only share in that glory through death. Both these losses shocked Georgy deeply.

Georgy, together with the rest of the people of Brussels, waited in trepidation for further news of her friends and relations. It was not long before they began to receive the dead, dying and wounded from the battlefields. Each litter that was bought in bore testament to the appalling injuries inflicted by shot and bayonet. Georgy anxiously looked for people she knew but often the faces were so disfigured and covered in blood it was hard to make out their identities. She later wrote: 'the first sight of the poor wounded was sickening, and each litter as it came into the town, filled us with intense anxiety to know whom it contained.'[88] The wait went on and the sisters busied themselves by spending long hours tending to the wounded and sending messages to the other families waiting for news. They also spent time scraping lint to dress the wounds of the injured and prepared cherry water in the kitchens of their house which they took to the makeshift tents used to house the wounded.

Georgy still found time to write reports to her aunt, whose son Lord Apsley was present at the battle. She reports on the status of her friends and her worries for her family:

> 'My dearest Georgy, [her aunt was also known by this name] I cannot write an amusing letter as I am in a horrid fuss at this general move, poor dear March I am frightened for. Prinny [the Prince of Orange, for whom March was A.D.C.] is such a foolish headstrong little fellow that I tremble he will get them into some scrape. We will write whenever we hear of dear Tim, he is extremely pleased with a letter he has received from Lord Bathurst and a great coat from my Aunt- God bless you.
>
> The garrison were under arms all last night and I hear so many drums and such a noise that I think they must be marching. I am afraid we are just near enough to hear the cannonading which I think will just kills us with anxiety.
>
> The Duke has gone off but is expected to return this evening. George [Lennox] is gone with him. Apsley [eldest son of Lord Bathurst] is still here, his horses are not arrived.'[89]

On 17th June Georgy found time to scribble another few lines to her aunt to inform her that thankfully most of their friends and all of their family were safe. Very little information had reached them about what exactly had taken place on the battlefield but the little she did know she recounted to Lady Bathurst:

> 'Thank God, my dearest G., all our friends are safe. There was a general action yesterday evening, the Guards were not engaged. George was sent galloping over the country and desired to meet the Duke here, so he was not in it. Poor Sir D. Pack is severely wounded and the poor Duke of Brunswick died of his wounds. The Belgian cavalry behaved gallantly, the infantry fled the field. The Duke is now pursuing them, but, thank God, we do not hear any cannons, which we did distinctly yesterday evening. The Prussians are come up, so if Bony is not soon annihilated I shall be surprised. The Scots were chiefly engaged, so there are no officers wounded that one knows. Apsley and George [Lennox] left us this morning very early. You cannot imagine our delight yesterday at seeing George arrive, it seemed so extraordinary to hear him talk of the balls that had been whizzing round him in the skirmish they had had. The Duke's baggage is still here, so I suppose he will not go far to-day. I hope you will not be in a fuss, we will let you know by every opportunity. G. saw Tim yesterday marching in perfect health. God bless you.'[90]

On 18th June Wellington rode back to the battlefield. Despite the claims made amongst the British families in Brussels that the Duke had been beaten, the outcome of the battle still hung in the balance and Wellington had not given up hope. Many civilians had fled to Antwerp, but the Lennoxes and most of their friends stayed. Georgy and her sisters wanted to help in whatever way they could and stayed so they could tend to the injured. However, there was a real anxiety as to what would happen if the French were to break through and take Brussels. Looting, pillage and rape were the norm for a victorious army and the British inhabitants could expect little mercy if the Allies were defeated. The Lennox sisters were assured that they would be spared this bloodthirsty treatment but the threats must have seemed very real to them. Wellington had personally assured the Lennox family that he would inform them if the battle was lost. Their luggage was packed so that they could leave with only a quarter of an hours warning.

Georgy and her sisters spent most of that third day walking in the park. Here they were more likely to see people they knew who may be able to share news of their family and friends. They walked the short distance to the house of a close friend, the Marquise D'Asche, on the corner of the park and the rue de la Pepiniere. From there they had a direct view of the wounded being brought back from the battlefield. Georgy, desperate for news, ran up to a group of wounded officers who were able to tell her that her brothers had once again escaped danger.

From the house they saw Lord Fitzroy Somerset and the Prince of Orange being brought in on stretchers, both seriously injured. Somerset had to have an arm amputated and after the grisly procedure was completed, he called for his severed arm to be brought back as he was desperate not to lose his wedding ring. He had recently married the bewitching Emily Wellesley-Pole, one of Wellington's nieces. Emily was heavily pregnant during this ordeal, but showed great strength of character throughout, prompting Georgy to note that she had 'shown a good deal of proper feeling on this occasion and [has] not been full of foolish fears and alarms. I admire her very much, she is looking so ill, poor thing.'[91]

Georgy now saw the Prince of Orange who told her that when he had been hit, March had leapt forward to help at great risk to his own personal safety. Before the Prince could be stretchered off the battlefield, March tore the cockade from the Prince's hat which had identified him as Royalty. The Prince was thereafter indebted to March as he always said that this precaution saved his life.[92] A bullet had pierced 'Prinny's' shoulder, taking weeks to work itself to the surface. It was

3. The Château d'Hougoumont, a photograph taken when Georgy and William later visited the site where the Battle of Waterloo had taken place.

however a battle wound of which he could be proud, having proved his worth on the battlefield at last. Weeks later he was still recovering, as reported by Charlotte Greville: 'Our heroic little Prince is very weak and looking very ill, I am afraid he will never recover the use of his arm and he suffers very much at times when pieces of bone come out. What does Princess Charlotte say to his feats?'[93], perhaps hopeful that the romance would now be rekindled between the Prince and the heiress to the throne.

That afternoon Richmond and William Pitt Lennox rode out to meet the Army on the outskirts of the battle. Wellington would not let them remain there as it was too dangerous so they returned to their family that evening, 'with good news that all was going on as well as possible.'[94] News then became more plentiful. George Lennox appeared at the house with orders from the Duke. He was full of excitement, exclaiming that bullets had been flying around him all morning.[95] The day was not without its surprises. Georgy wrote:

> 'We had had a fearful alarm during the day, as the Cumberland Hussars (a Hanovarian Regiment) came full gallop through Brussels, saying that the allied army was defeated and that the French were arriving in the town. But before long the truth was known, and not much credit was given to the story that these Hussars had been pursued; the facts being that, upon hearing the whistle of shots about their ears, they had wheeled round and trotted off from the field!'[96]

Soon after the battle this regiment was disbanded for cowardice.

Wellington was, as history records, the hero of the hour. He was everywhere at once, anywhere he was needed, whether to give an order or encouragement to his men. He galloped from regiment to regiment on his faithful Copenhagen who did not tire or falter. Wellington searched the horizon for the Prussians as his Allied forces had been terribly weakened by the onslaught and would not be able to hold for much longer. Several hours later he finally he spotted Bücher's army through his telescope. One of the Duke's A.D.C.s called out: 'The day is our own! The Prussians have arrived!'[97] Relief and joy flooded those who heard his words and the news spread quickly throughout the ranks of soldiers. Wellington even allowed himself an uncharacteristic show of enthusiasm, pulling off his hat and waving it at the French, encouraging the last divisions to sweep the enemy one last time and see them home. The danger was however far from over. Lord Uxbridge, on horseback alongside the Duke, was hit by a shot which narrowly missed Copenhagen's neck. 'By God! I've lost my leg!' he exclaimed in surprise. 'Have you, by God!'[98] replied Wellington, supporting his friend in the saddle until he could be helped off his horse and carried away. But Wellington himself refused to fall back to a safer position until the battle was over, claiming: 'The battle's won, my life's no consequence now.'[99]

Meanwhile Napoleon fled the battlefield in a carriage that was later captured by the returning and vengeful Prussians. They are said to have found inside one million francs worth of diamonds and a cake of Windsor soap.[100] The man himself had escaped on horseback, reaching his headquarters at Charleroi the next morning. As Napoleon fled, Wellington met with Blücher outside the Belle-Alliance Inn on the road to Brussels. The two veterans shook hands and victory was formerly declared. After the meeting the Duke rode back through the dark, witnessing the shadows of destruction that was left in the wake of the battle. The stark reality of the number of men they had lost now hit Wellington. The Duke gazed over the fields of bodies, the ground awash with blood, flesh and scraps of uniform. William Pitt Lennox also remembered encountering:

> 'dead, dying or wounded men. Many a familiar acquaintance gave us a ghastly recognition, as the wretched sufferer was

> being carried to the rear, shot or pierced through the body by bullet or lance; many a brave comrade opened his eyes for a moment, as the clattering of our horses' feet attracted his attention, to close them again in death; and many a gay, thoughtless stripling, who, within four short days, had been a guest at my mother's ball in Brussels, was now stretched in death on the ensanguined turf.'[101]

When Dr Hume read out the official list of dead to the Duke, it is reported that he wept openly. How could he celebrate this victory when the loss had been so very great? However, without a doubt, without the Duke's tenacity, victory could easily have escaped them. That afternoon the debt owed to Wellington weighed heavily on everyone's minds.

As the Lennox family sat down to dinner that evening a messenger arrived with the news that Napoleon had been defeated. Georgy wrote that: 'brilliant victory was known...and most thankful we were that our immediate belongings had been mercifully protected, and that war was at an end, although the losses were fearfully great.'[102] In fact Georgy was lucky that most of her closest friends and all of her relatives who had been involved in the fighting had survived. Witnessing the shocking realities of war through the eyes of the injured and dying men returning to Brussels had served as a brutal initiation into adult life for Georgy. It was a world away from the privileged lifestyle which was all she had ever known and her life would be profoundly changed from this moment onwards.

On 19th June Wellington returned to Brussels, mentally and physically exhausted. He had barely slept as his bed had been occupied by his close friend Sir Alexander Gordon who was slowly dying of his injuries. Wellington had stayed up attempting to write his official dispatch of the battle to send back to England. As Gordon's groans grew worse the Duke could bear it no longer and took himself and his half written dispatch to Brussels. Holed up in his house on the rue de la Montagne du Parc, he was called upon by Richmond. He and Georgy were taking a walk in the park having heard that Wellington was back from the front. The Duke joined them in the park and Georgy noted: 'He looked very sad, and when we shook hands with him and congratulated him, he said, "It is a dearly bought victory. We have lost so many fine fellows."[103] As he said earlier 'It has been a damned serious business. Blücher and I have lost 30,000 men. It has been a damned nice thing- the nearest run thing you ever saw in your life.'[104] Richmond asked him to dinner, but his offer was refused. Wellington had many matters to attend to and wanted to dine alone.

Soon news reached Brussels that Alexander Gordon had died. Lord Apsley informed his mother Lady Bathurst by letter, remarking that he had been 'vastly active and alive in the field, and would, I am sure, have been an excellent officer.'[105] Sarah Lennox wrote to her cousin Lady Georgina Bathurst:

> 'I am grieved to tell you about poor Colonel Gordon, as I know you will be very much shocked. His leg was taken off, but he did not survive it. Lord F. Somerset is doing very well; he has lost his right arm...We have just seen the Duke; he told us he thought there would be no more fighting...All the English are gone here. You have no idea what we have suffered- hearing the cannonading and seeing the wounded.'[106]

Even Charlotte Greville was moved. She wrote that: 'There are too many to deplore, but there is not one more regretted as our poor friend

Alex Gordon. He was universally beloved here, indeed it was impossible knowing him well not to esteem and to be attached to him. I hope he did not suffer much, as he was so much exhausted by loss of blood that he fell asleep and waked no more.'[107]

The next day the Richmond family was reunited with March who had escaped the battle unscathed. A few weeks later, Georgy wrote to her cousin: 'Think of our delight at seeing the Duke the day after the victory, and dear March the following day. It made up for all the misery we had endured.'[108] She continued that it was:

> 'Poor Lord Hay that I regret the most- but there is no use entering upon such melancholy subjects. I have been out every day in fear and trembling in case of meeting Lord Hotham amongst the wounded. I long to nurse even the poor privates. We have several people we know wounded here, all slightly. It is such a pleasure to be useful to them now, poor creatures. Lady C. Capel has seen Ld Uxbridge; he is recovering. Poor Ld F. Somerset is low at having lost his arm; he says all his prospects in life are blighted…'[109]

Lord Uxbridge's lost leg did not diminish his sense of spirit. Seymour Bathurst reported to his father Lord Bathurst that Uxbridge was in high spirits, saying: 'it is fair that he should no longer cut the young men out as a handsome, well made fellow, which he has done for many years.'[110]

The next day Wellington left Brussels for Orville and by the middle of the next month he was in Paris where he had many matters to attend to. The Duke had proved himself worthy of the accolades and honours loaded on him after his adventures in the peninsular. He had almost singlehandedly saved the Allied forces from a crushing defeat which would have plunged them once again into a state of open warfare against Napoleon. He was the undisputed hero of the hour. He said at the time: 'I hope to God, that I have fought my last battle. It is a bad thing to be always fighting. While in the thick of it, I am much too occupied to feel anything; but it is wretched just after. It is quite impossible to think of glory. Both mind and feeling are exhausted.'[111] This indeed would be Wellington's last battle, as he wished. Napoleon surrendered himself to the mercy of the English hoping for exile in England. Instead he was sent to the remote island of St. Helena and with no hope of escape, he remained there until his death in 1821.

In the weeks following the battle, the wounded still required constant attention and many women were returning to Brussels to tend to their relatives. The infamous Lady Caroline Lamb, ex-lover of Lord Byron, arrived to nurse her popular and attractive brother Colonel Frederick Ponsonby. Georgy, who greatly disliked Caroline Lamb, reported to her aunt that: 'Ponsonby is doing well, but she [Lady Caroline] will hurt him I fear. The surgeon told her the best thing she could do would be to hold her tongue; in answer to her wishing to know if she had not better read to him all day.'[112] Lady Caroline was well-known for her wild behaviour and sharp tongue having been brought up in the company of her aunt the Duchess of Devonshire and the infamous Devonshire House set. Fortunately, Colonel Ponsonby was quick to recover, with or without his sister's help. On 3rd July it was recorded that 'Fred Ponsonby is the only one who has given me any anxiety and he is improving so rapidly it is quite delightful.'[113]

Lady De Lancey, who had been sent to Antwerp for safety, had been told that her husband had been killed, but this was not true and he had in fact been stretchered off the battlefield and was slowing dying in the village of Waterloo itself. After a few days Lady De Lancey was finally brought to him and cared for him tenderly for several painful days during his slow demise. They had only been married a matter of months and the pair had proved a charming and popular addition to the Brussels social scene. Her plight had caught the imagination of many who had heard her sad tale and she became well known for it. Georgy was perhaps a little jealous of Lady de Lancey. She wrote to Lady Bathurst how:

> 'Sir W. Delancey is dead, after all. I cannot say I felt much pity for her [Lady de Lancey] which seems inhuman, but she really must be composed of flint. Lady Hamilton having heard he was killed and Lady Delancey having no friend [to tell her], she went to break it to her in Antwerp, she prepared her by saying he was badly wounded. Lady Delancey, extremely angry, said she wished people would keep their reports to themselves, she felt sure he was safe, and the following morning they heard he was not killed but wounded, and Lady Hamilton after repeated entreaties prevailed on Lady Delancey to come to Brussels and from there she went to Waterloo, she wrote a most extraordinary letter before he died, saying she wished General Dundas would go to her as she wished to settle several things relative to his internment. Can you conceive it, and requesting General Dundas to take her to England when her husband was dead. At Antwerp she said to Lady Hamilton: "I have had little enough of matrimony. I have only been married 9 weeks". I hope I may never see her.'[114]

When Lady De Lancey wrote down her experiences of those days she portrayed herself as a victim of tragic circumstances, doing all she could for her dying husband. She obviously failed to convince Georgy, although she certainly melted the hearts of many others.

With the battle now safely behind them and their friendship renewed, Georgy was again absorbed by the particular attention paid to her by the Duke of Wellington. On 28th June he wrote from Paris regarding the miniature of himself by Rochard which he had given Georgy the night before the battle. Georgy had spent the evenings in the weeks after the battle working up an embroidered sash to send him, whilst enquiring about having copies made of the miniature she had been given. The Duke replied: 'My Dearest Georgy, I am very much obliged to you for the embroidery. If you give your picture, the painter will change it, therefore you should sit with it while he copies it. We are getting on delightfully.'[115] When Georgy enquired how many copies she could request from Rochard, he replied 'Dearest Georgy, Many thanks for your letter of the 6th. I don't care how many Copies the Painter makes of the picture. As you liked it, however, I recommended it to you not to trust it in his hands. I do invite you to Paris. Your brothers are quite well. I saw William [Pitt Lennox] last night; such a buck, I should not have known him.'[116]

Georgy was rightly very proud to have received letters from Wellington at such a busy time, as she then reported to her aunt: 'I had a note from the Duke of Wellington the other day of the 28th from Orville. I have been extremely grand with it, I assure you...'[117] It is easy to imagine Georgy showing off the letter to her sisters and friends. Wellington was now in Paris, together with many of the young men who had also been at Waterloo, all of whom were keen to celebrate their victory over Napoleon in style. Wellington invited Georgy to join them and she responded positively. She included in her reply a good dose of gossip and perhaps requested a lock of hair from the Duke, which he was happy to provide:

'Dearest Georgy, I received your letter of the 27th. and I now send you a bit of my precious hair. I am much obliged to you for the information about the Guards! I was not aware of what you tell me. Let me hear from you sometimes and & Believe me. Ever Yours Most Affectionately. '[118]

Giving a lock of hair was an intimate gesture, indicating the level of affectionate flirtation that now existed between Georgy and the Duke. Although Wellington's giving female friends locks of his hair was common in the latter years of his life, this occasion is exceptionally rare as it is the only known example from the time of the Battle of Waterloo. Georgy kept the hair in its original envelope with Wellington's other letters in a hand sewn pouch for the rest of her life. The significance of this gesture could be just that of a gentleman to his young female friend- nothing more- but no doubt Georgy felt it was a sign of something special. Her crush on the Duke had not abated despite the attentions of other men and no doubt this gesture fanned those flames of affection. For Wellington's part, both the giving of the miniature and the lock of hair can be seen as uncharacteristically sentimental, perhaps a sign of his increased sensitivity in the wake of what he had just been through.

The majority of these days in Brussels were spent visiting the wounded and running errands for them. However, taking visitors to the fields where the battle had taken place soon became a fashionable pastime. Georgy herself went on several occasions, sending a cockade to her cousin Lady Georgina that she had cut off one of the French caps in the field. The ground was littered with debris from the battle including bits of uniform, bone and cannon shot.

The Lennox family now made plans for their next move. No more letters between Georgy and Wellington survive from the remaining time that she spent in Brussels, possibly because she destroyed them due to their content; but more probably because Wellington was too busy for a continuous correspondence at this time. Staying in Brussels had been a formative experience for Georgy. She had grown in confidence, socialised with men who desired her for more than just her innocent charms and aristocratic background, and she had even succeeded at times to escape the overbearing presence of her mother. Georgy and her sisters were well and truly initiated into Wellington's inner circle of friends. Few were lucky enough to be in this position, to enjoy his confidences and to share in his rare moments of despair. Witnessing first-hand the horrors of war in the injuries of those carried back from the battlefield must have been a sobering experience for the young Georgy. Her front row seat and close friendship and flirtation with Wellington gave her a feeling of great pride. Being his favourite Lennox sister allowed her to stand proud and stand out from her many sisters. Her relationship with Wellington was on course to flourish and to endure for many years to come.

CHAPTER FIVE

Riding the Coach

'We shall have famous sport when the Lennox's come, and I will not fail to send you a bulletin'[119]

John Freemantle

After the excesses and extremes of life in the ballroom and on the battlefield the Duke of Richmond and his family felt the need for a change. The Duke, together with Mary and Georgy, left Brussels in early August to spend a few weeks in Spa, famous for its revitalising cold springs and mineral waters. Richmond also felt he needed a few weeks respite from his wife. Rumours of the Duchess's extravagant spending and gambling debts were by now well-known. One report claimed, 'that the D. of R. is a completely ruined Man, & has no prospects of ever being able to return to England, that the Dss has been gambling in Paris & elsewhere.'[120]

Sussex, one of the younger Lennox sons, was in poor health, so their tutor Spencer Madan took him and two of the other younger boys to Ostend to take the waters there. Sarah Lennox and March were left behind in Brussels with the Duchess with whom they got on 'tolerably well.'[121] The parties continued but were greatly diminished in frequency and in size due to the number of injured soldiers. The plan for the family was to be reunited in Brussels after their various trips, before heading to Paris to join Wellington and his other staff officers, but this did not work out as expected.

Sarah, like Georgy, had been having her own fair share of romantic adventures and over the previous few months she had been growing ever closer to General Maitland, for whom March had been a valued A.D.C. She had even asked Georgina Bathurst for her opinion of him. In Sarah's next reply to her cousin she wrote 'I am delighted at what you tell me about your friend Genl. Maitland; I am sure he deserves all the praise; he is a most delightful person, and I am sure you and Aunt B. will be quite captivated by him. He has sent me a Legion of Honor taken by his Brigade of Guards at Waterloo, which I am very proud of.'[122] Sarah had convinced her parents to allow her to stay in Brussels which allowed her to spend more time with Maitland, a relationship which had continued to blossom unnoticed by either the Duke or Duchess.

After the chaos of war torn Brussels, Spa was a peaceful idyll but Georgy was excited to get to Paris and join Wellington and his 'family' of staff officers. By the middle of October the Duke and Duchess of

Richmond and their four eldest daughters had been reunited and arrived in Paris together. They intended to stay for at least a month and then return to Brussels to relieve Spencer who was not making much progress in his attempts to tame the youngest Lennox boys. Spencer reported home that there had been 'no end to their riots, let alone their pilfering the store room, thrashing the maids, and sending out for red herring & gin.'[123] He continued that the younger Lennox girls were being cared for by a rather wild ladies maid 'who dresses them, and hears them their lessons', but who spent 'a great deal of company with the butler, and very little with the ladies.'[124]

The Duchess returned to Brussels to try to take back control of her unruly children but the other three remained in Paris when Georgy fell dangerously ill with typhus. Spencer had been informed by the family of the news but was quick to report his disbelief that Georgy was really ill: 'It seems that Genl. Barnes was to give a grand ball on their account on Wednesday, for which they were however induced to stay'. In the same letter Spencer wrote that 'Lady Georgiana had been confined two days to her bed by a violent cold, and yet I would bet any wager that she went to the ball. She had always appeared to me to be very delicate, and will very probably fall an early victim to fashionable dissipation.'[125] Indeed, Georgy was delicate although her love for balls was by no means unusual for a woman of her age and rank. Luckily for Georgy social events continued in the same way in Paris as they had in Brussels before Waterloo. Georgy hated missing events but this illness was severe and she was confined to her bed for many weeks; missing out on many of the balls.

In his next letter home Spencer was forced to concede that, 'unfortunately Lady Georgiana Lennox had had a severe attack of cold and fever, which obliged her to keep her bed: according to the last accounts she was better, but still unable to get up, or leave her bed longer than whilst it was made. In all probability she will not regain her strength so as to undertake the journey before the spring.'[126] Georgy was indeed very ill. Yet her spirits were buoyed by her ongoing relationship with Wellington. Although he was as busy as ever with official functions and the business of organising the Army of Occupation in France, he arranged to have Georgy sent her dinner every day and made time to see her on any occasion she was well enough to receive a visitor. As her strength grew Wellington sent one of his carriages for her to be driven around in so she could take some air.

Such kind attentions would not have gone unnoticed. Anxious to see their daughter returned to full health, the Duke and Duchess must have felt honoured that Georgy was held in such high regard by Wellington. Wellington sent Georgy a shawl to cheer her up and insisted that she attend a ball he was giving at the Elysée Bourbon. Georgy was still very weak and bound to a wheelchair but could not refuse such an offer. She did attend and was no doubt delighted with the attention she received as a temporary invalid. This particularly extravagant ball was one of the Duke's last hurrahs in Paris before leaving for Cambrai where his military quarters were to be based. The Duchess of Wellington was also in Paris at this time but was not enjoying the social scene as Georgy was. She wrote: 'of Paris there is not much to say. There is no society of French, nor any amusement except what the theatres afford. There are, however, many of these, and most of them very gay, and we go to one almost every night after the play, which everybody goes to, and nobody likes, for it is indeed very dull.'[127] The Duchess's relationship with Wellington was still difficult, but the two put on a united front as they attended many events thrown in the Duke's honour to celebrate his victory at Waterloo.

In October the family discovered that Sarah had eloped with General Maitland which came as a shock as their courtship had gone largely unnoticed. Maitland had been a close friend of the family in Brussels and had more than proven his worth during the Battle of Waterloo for which had been awarded the Order of the Bath. This however was not enough for the Duke of Richmond who had had in mind for Sarah the heir to a family dynasty like his own. Although Maitland was well liked, in the Duke's opinion his lack of pedigree disqualified him from the race for Sarah's hand. Richmond never imagined that his daughter would risk it all and run away with a man she loved hoping to complete the ceremony before they were discovered. There was much excitement in the house that day when Sarah was discovered to be missing, her sisters could not believe that she had gone to such lengths to be with Maitland. Although Georgy had known of her sister's love, she was shocked to discover what she had done.

The thrilling story of their adventure was later told by the rather disapproving Reverend Somerset, Chaplain of the Guards Division. The Reverend had been disturbed in the middle of his evening meal by a messenger at his door. He was taken to where Maitland and Sarah were waiting in their coach, 'She was sobbing aloud, 'He we are'- said the General- 'We have just ran away from the Duke's- we shall be pursued- will you marry us instantly'. Somerset refused because they did not have the necessary permission of the Commander-in-Chief, Wellington.'[128] After some undignified pleading the couple left, driving through the night to try to find a man in holy orders who would marry them. Getting increasingly desperate, they returned to

Reverend Somerset at dawn, who was unbending. He insisted that they get permission from Wellington.

Sarah's reputation was now in tatters, having run away from home and spent the night in a carriage with a man who was not her husband. As Wellington took his breakfast he was told what had happened. He quickly went to call on Somerset who reported that the Duke received him with an 'overbearing stare and abrupt questioning... he [Wellington] gave his consent, because I believe he had talk'd the thing over with the Duke of Richmond, [and] desired me to prepare the license in his private room...and marry General Maitland on his arrival'. Somerset concluded that Wellington was indeed 'a man who will serve his friends at all costs.'[129] The short marriage ceremony was completed in Wellington's headquarters with the Duke as a witness. Exhausted but exonerated, General Maitland and his new wife now had to face the wrath of the Duke of Richmond. As the elopement had ended honourably and having been secured by the family's good friend Wellington, the Duke's anger quickly abated. Like Jane Austen's Mr. Darcy, the Duke had brought about a quick marriage to secure the reputation of his friends showing how committed he was to the happiness and success of the Lennox family.

In the end Wellington's intervention was fortuitous, as the family came out in full support for Sarah and exclaimed their delight at the match. The Reverend concluded:

> 'It turns out to be the luckiest thing in the world for them that I made so many difficulties; as it gave them time for her Papa's anger to cool and for the Duke of Wellington to take advantage of his actually good nature and affection for his family. I was quite sure from the first moment, that the Duchess [of

> Richmond], her mama, as a Complete woman of the world would face the thing, probably say the General was her great favourite in all the world, and that how it was a pity that when people are in love they will not want to let thing work their way quietly, but take such violent and odd measures in their hands! Things took just their course. Four days after the Wedding the Bride returned to the World! Made her debut at a grand family dinner, all branches delighted; and nothing was heard of for a week after but the Ambassador was to give the married couple a dinner such a day, Lord Castlereagh such a day, the Duke of Wellington such a day, &c, &c...The Duke of Richmond, however, is in spite of all these gaieties, sensibly hurt; and he said to me with some emphasis and significance, he had been long enough in Paris and wish'd himself back, and in Brussels.'[130]

The Lennox family never did return to Brussels as they had planned. They remained in Paris over the winter until early in 1816 when Georgy was considered well enough to return to England. She wrote to Wellington to inform him that she had arrived safely back in London. Her recovery had been painfully slow and to her horror, the doctors had insisted that she shave her head to prevent her fever from returning. Wellington wrote to her 'Dearest Georgy, Many thanks for your letter; and I am delighted to find that you have performed your journey so well. You must take care of yourself and keep yourself warm during the Winter. I dont agree with the Barber about your Hair. All his frizzling will not preclude the necessity of your being shaved. There is nothing new here. Ever Yours Most Affecy.[131] The following month he wrote again 'Dearest Georgy, I have received your letter of the 31st. and am glad to find you are getting well. You must still take care you yourself however till the spring is well advanced. You say nothing of your hair, which I conclude is shaved off.'[132]

By the summer Georgy was full recovered and her hair had grown back sufficiently for her to return to society. Wellington was still in Paris having spent some time in Cheltenham before heading back to Cambrai where the Army of Occupation was stationed. He wrote to her from Paris in June, still concerned as ever for her wellbeing and approval, this time on a house he hoped to rent: 'Dearest Georgy, I have received your letter for which I am much obliged to you. I have not yet got Mme. Gougons answer about Mont St. Martin [where he hoped to rent]; but I shall be very much disappointed if I dont get the house; and you dont come to see me in it. I hear you stayed till past four at the Ball on the Kings Birthday.'[133] Luckily Wellington did manage to let the house in Mont St. Martin which would prove to be the perfect house for many a wild party that Georgy attended. That Georgy stayed until past four at the Kings birthday ball shows that she had fully recovered and was back on the London scene with gusto. Wellington's comment about this hints of a fatherly rebuke as he gently reminds Georgy of her recent ill health.

After the Battle of Waterloo, Cambray (or Cambrai as it is now known) was for three years the base of the Army of Occupation, led by Wellington. It was close to Paris and attracted a milieu of young women who stayed to socialise with the military staff based there. After the prolonged horrors of the Peninsular War and the Hundred Days ending at the Battle of Waterloo, the Army had only their regimental and ceremonial duties to attend to; so there was plenty of time for parties.

Still confined to London however, Georgy was keen to have her own fun and began an affair with a gentleman mysteriously referred to as 'The Soupriant' in letters between herself and Wellington. The name, which simply means 'suitor' could be applied to many of the men with whom Georgy flirted and danced with during this time. However, it is likely that the Soupriant was Lord Rous, later the 2nd Earl of Stradbroke. No doubt Georgy enjoyed the Lord Rous's attentions after her long illness. Perhaps there was also a desire to show Wellington, far away in France, that she was attractive, and attracted, to other men. Her own mother was certainly taken in by the courtship and was keen to see her daughter married to Rous. At one of the many balls attended by the Duchess of Richmond and her daughters, the Duchess was being escorted down the ballroom's main staircase by Captain Lindsay, whilst Georgy was on the arm of 'the Soupriant'. The Duchess began 'walking quick and looking somewhat agitated', trying to give the two young lovers some space to themselves. She exclaimed to Lindsay:

> 'Oh! I see it will do Capt. Lindsay I see it will do!' to which Lindsay responded
>
> 'What will do Ma'am? I dont know what you mean!'
>
> 'Oh! I see that you are not in on the secret! You dont know! But I see it will do, that's all!'[134]

The Duchess was delighted at the match she could see forming.

Wellington wrote to Georgy about this incident which had been recounted to him personally by Captain Lindsay. Through Lindsay he had heard the rumour of her impending betrothal to the Soupirant and demanded to know 'How is this?' There is no surviving letter to show how Georgy responded to this probe for information.

By September Wellington was well adjusted to life in Cambrai. His position was comfortable and opportunities to socialise were plentiful. He found time to entertain on a regular basis, welcoming old friends and new to dine at his table. The evenings were raucous, with much flirting and fun between the young staff officers and their visiting ladies. He wrote to Georgy, 'I am going to Alsace on Tuesday [to] Review the troops and I shall be back about the 28 or 29th. By that time I conclude that the Duke [of Richmond] and all of you will be on your return from Aubigny [the Richmonds' estate in France, where they had gone for a short visit]. Your sister [now Lady Sarah Maitland] has just dined with us, and is remarkably well. She looks better than she did when I was here in Spring.'[135] Marriage certainly suited Sarah but Georgy would not be swayed when it came to bring things with Rous to a conclusion; in any case she was much too excited about returning to Wellington's side at Cambrai. Despite her mother's ambitions Georgy did not marry Rous: the courtship was mere diversion and no engagement was ever formally announced.

In October Georgy finally re-joined Wellington and they immediately renewed their close companionship. The prosperity of peacetime allowed for past traditions to be resurrected with new enthusiasm. Military reviews were once again a common occurrence with many female companions brought along for the day out. Freemantle, one of Wellington's staff officers who wrote revealing letters home to his parents, reported on how the groups would travel:

> 'the party in the duke's carriage [was] always Felton & his wife, & Poole, or some other youth (a visitor). The Duchess of Wellington always took the Duchess of Richmond, our Lady Lennox & Lady Edward Somerset. Lady Angelsey and ladies

> went in their own carriage. The Duke always went to ground with Mrs Hervey, Lady Georgina [sic] Lennox & Lady Jane Paget at his side, the two former always close to him.'[136]

Georgy once again rode out with the Duke to his reviews, as she had done in Ireland and at Waterloo, which allowed her to bask in the pleasure of being Wellington's chosen companion. An excellent horsewoman herself, Georgy was permitted to ride Copenhagen, who had carried Wellington to victory on the fields of Waterloo. There were also the occasional re-enactments of battles to amuse the staff officers. Georgy later wrote that:

> 'one morning [Wellington] announced that there was to be a sham fight, and that he had given orders to Sir G. Scovell that the ladies riding should be taken prisoners, so he recommended our keeping close to him. I had no difficulty in doing so, as I was riding Copenhagen and I found myself the only one with him in a square, where they were firing. To the Duke's great amusement we heard one of the soldiers saying to another "Take care of that 'ere horse, he kicks out; we knew him well in Spain," pointing to Copenhagen! He was a most unpleasant horse to ride, but always snorted and neighed with pleasure at the sight of troops.'[137]

On one occasion in October 1817 when Georgy was riding Copenhagen at one of the reviews, she jumped a ditch, the stirrup broke and she fell off. Georgy always later told this story as a rather amusing incident, glossing over her evident embarrassment at the time. Her falling off brought the entire Review to a halt in front of various foreign dignitaries with everyone scrambling to help Georgy regain her seat. That evening she attended a dance organised by the Duke. He came up to her, sensing her embarrassment from earlier in the day and wanting to make her laugh, he exclaimed: 'Here's the heroine of the day! Got kicked off and didn't mind it!'[138] Which of course thrilled Georgy.

However Freemantle gives a rather different description of the event:

> 'The last day a ridiculous circumstance occurred; as we were going down the line, ADCs preceding etc in grand parade, Lady Georgina's stirrup broked [sic] as her horse was going over the little ditch and she slipt [sic] off, but the duke & Lord Lyndoch dismounted, and the whole cavalcade was stopt [sic] until the groom brought another stirrup leather; there were present by special invitation, the Austrian, Russian, and Prussian commanders in chief and a prodigious number of foreigners of all nations.'[139]

Boar hunting was another popular pastime for the Duke and his circle of friends and Georgy would often ride as cover for the main party. Even when she was not present, the subject still provided content for the Duke's letters to her: 'We have had but bad hunting since you went; but the weather appears to be becoming more favourable and I hope for some sport tomorrow.'[140] On another occasion Georgy rode with the Duke's hunting party when he caught an enormous boar, 'of which feat he was prouder than of Waterloo! He was very anxious to show me the boar, and I was equally anxious not to see it, and Sir George Murray helped me to avoid the unpleasant sight. The boar's bristles were given to me, and were mounted for me by Lord Arthur Hill, A.D.C. to the Duke, with an inscription.'[141] The mounted bristles are still in the possession of Georgy's descendants.

The parties, rumours and romances continued but for Georgy it was still Colonel Felton Hervey-Bathurst who held her main affection. One evening in October 1816, Georgy's jealousy of Felton talking with her sister Jane bubbled over. She exclaimed to the Duke 'Why don't you make your aid de camp treat your company with more respect?' to which he replied good humouredly 'why don't you both fall upon him, you then would surely be more than a match for him [!]'[142]

Of all the riotous entertainments, the Duke's favourite 'sport' was a rather wild game called 'Riding the Coach' which was possibly of his own invention. Georgy recalled that there 'were long corridors at Mont St. Martin; along these they [Wellington and his staff officers] dragged ladies on rugs, the gentlemen being harnessed, and called it riding the coach.'[143] Wellington wrote to Georgy: 'Our Richard and Lady were here on Sunday last. He was assez comique. We gave her a ride in the coach. I was Coachman and her fright was capital. We have not had any ladies since, but I believe Lady Sarah [Maitland] will come this week and I expect Lady Asgill will call on her way from Paris.'[144] The following month another letter arrived from the Duke regaling a tale of this evening activity with the added dimension of harnessed goats:

> 'We are going on as usual. Riding in the Coach, dancing the Mazurka &c&c. The house is as full as it can hold. Yesterday was a very bad day, and I went to Cambray, and I understand that they hunted Lord C- through all the corridors, even that in the roof. At night we had an improvement on the coach. Two goats were brought in and harnessed, but instead of being horses, and assisting to draw, they chose to lie down and be drawn. The night before, the ladies drew me the petty tour [the shorter route through the corridors] and afterward Lord Hill the grand tour, but the 'fat, fair and forty' [Lord Hill], and M [Marchioness of Conyngham] were so knocked up that some of us were obliged to go into the harness, although we

> had already run many stages, and to draw Lord Hill on.'[145]

The image of Wellington cavorting through the corridors of the house roaring with laughter and dragging women on rugs behind him is quite at odds with the universal image of him as a strict and humourless disciplinarian. In truth, around his friends and in the safety of life away from the public gaze, Wellington was fun-loving, caring and kind-hearted with a wicked and playful sense of humour to match Georgy's.

Wellington was known for always keeping his friends in his thoughts and took delight in marital match-making although his own marriage still proved disappointing; indeed Kitty spent many months away from Cambrai where she did not feel particularly welcome. The Duke even tried to match-make for Georgy's brother William Pitt Lennox: 'I advised Wm. [Lennox] to cut Miss Newcastle and pay court to one of the large fortunes here, to which he appeared rather inclined; but she keeps him still' William seems to have been caught under 'Miss Newcastle's' spell, although nothing more about her is known. With matchmaking there was inevitably some love-sickness, referred to as being 'poorly' in letters. It was a predicament suffered by many of Wellington's friends after the lovely Lennox sisters left Cambrai. Writing to Georgy, Wellington gossiped about 'poor Percy', who was 'very poorly for Lady Elizabeth Conyngham! Freemantle likewise is poorly; but you know for whom. He was very melancholy and gentlemanlike and by no means nimble on the Journey to London.'[146] As the Lennoxes packed their possessions to return to London, Freemantle confirmed that they would be missed, 'The Duchess of Richmond and the whole family left us on Friday last, much regretted, the old one for the constant sport she afforded, and the young ones for their amusement.'[147]

Back in London Georgy rekindled her affection for Lord Hotham, however the Duke still preferred Lord Rous. He wrote 'I have a very good opinion of him and wish that you liked him. I don't approve of you waiting for the Caprice of the Enemys Guardians' indicating that a proposal between Georgy and Hotham was finally on the cards. Hotham's parents refused to give consent to the match and without their financial aid a marriage was impossible. Although of impeccable breeding, this is evidence that Georgy was no longer considered a first-rate choice for marriage. The reality was that Georgy would only bring her pedigree to the marriage and no dowry. The Richmonds financial circumstances were such that they could not provide any money to their daughters when they married. In a similar way to Elizabeth Bennett in Pride and Prejudice, Georgy also had to contend with the wild reputation of her family including her unmanageable mother as well as her own love of late nights and balls. They declined to accept her for her many other qualities and the romance ended forthwith. Although this was another blow to Georgy and especially to her mother, Georgy and Hotham remained on friendly terms over the years. Georgy wrote to her mother many years later when Hotham was in ill health: 'I heard from Lord Hotham the other day, poor man he does seem to be feeling any better, tho' he says he is told his not being worse is a sign there is nothing so decidedly wrong.'[146a]

In 1817 Georgy turned twenty-two years old. Many of her friends and family members were married and beginning to start families. Georgy was faced with the prospect of either marrying for money and possibly being very unhappy or marrying for pleasure and greatly reducing her circumstances. Growing up in some of the most lavish residences in the country Georgy was fearful of leading a life away from the comforts of home and family. Yet she had also seen what could happen when a marriage was based on money and position, not love. Pressure to marry from her parents was growing stronger. That spring March had married Lady Caroline Paget, the daughter of Lord Anglesey. Now her favourite son was settled with an aristocratic wife the Duchess turned her attentions to her younger children and Georgy was the first to be targeted.

Georgy remained close to Wellington and their relationship continued in a flirtatious but ultimately caring manner. In 1817 they were both in Paris and began exchanging poetry, about which the Duke writes to her in January: 'My dearest Georgy, I hope soon to send you some more poetry notwithstanding that there is less leisure time for writing here than there was at the Abbaye [Cambrai]. I hear that a terrible accident happened to the last Poem.'[148] Possibly the accident was that it was read by of one of her sisters or perhaps even her mother, when it was supposed to be private. No poem survives, which is surprising given Georgy's tendency to hoard everything given to her by the Duke. A poem from the hand of the hero of Waterloo would certainly have done the rounds of her friends and relations, unless its contents were too intimate for drawing room conversation. Wellington always referred to Georgy as 'My Dearest Georgy' in all his letters to her, a very rare level of intimacy which he seldom used for either friend of family member. Whether their friendship 'tipped over' into something more ardent at this point is unknown, but even when the passions passed, and the friendship evolved, Wellington continued to reserve the accolade of 'my dearest' for Georgy alone.

Poems that were composed between the Duke and his officers as a joint effort were also mentioned in letters between them at this time which no doubt would have been shared and enjoyed between Georgy and her sisters. These would have been more innocent concoctions intended to delight and amuse the sisters. Between Georgy and Wellington his family of staff officers were christened 'the Poets'. In his next letter the Duke wrote 'Excepting Lord Arthur [Hill, an A.D.C.] the Poets are all so poorly [love-sick] that I dont believe much progress has yet been made in a new Poem but I'll take care that you shall have something for Valentines Day.'[149] The thought that the Duke of Wellington was sending her a Valentine's Day poem would have certainly thrilled Georgy, even if it was a jovial effort involving the staff officers- receiving such a poem marked her out against all of Wellington's other female friends. Sadly this poem too is lost which indicates its contents may have been too saucy to keep for posterity.

Unfortunately, at this time Georgy suffered an untimely relapse in the illness which had so troubled her in Paris. Wellington continued his correspondence and now wrote to her: 'I was very sorry to hear from the Duchess of your being unwell and I beg you let me know immediately how you are. I gave a most brilliant ball on the 29th. It wanted you only to be perfect. I want you likewise for another reason.'[150] Wellington goes on to say that at his ball he had played a favourite game of theirs which they had invented together. A 'fiction' or lie would be thought up between them and then told to their chosen victim. They would then sit back and wait to see how fast the rumour was circulated, a mark of how gossipy the person had been. It was, in effect, a kind of ballroom 'Chinese whispers'. Wellington wrote:

> 'Between ourselves entirely we have been playing the finest trick ever yet performed; and it is unfortunate that so capital

> an actress as you should be absent on this occasion. We really quite surpassed ourselves and in the best possible way the way which is my favourite one, viz founding our scheme on a fiction invented and circulated by the Person on whom the trick was played. We are not yet found out, which is fortunate. As you say "It would be a pity if you or I were ever discovered as we are so very innocent".'[151]

This letter is a lovely example of rapport between Georgy and the Duke, as well as evidence of the games and tricked they enjoyed by playing innocent and fooling others.

Despite her illness, The Soupriant, Lord Rous, was still persistent in his advances. Wellington wrote: 'I am glad to find the Soupriant R is getting on. I think there is no doubt of what he means, but you are quite right not to allow yourself to think of him until he will say what he means.'[152] Rous clearly had not explicitly proposed to Georgy yet, leaving her in an awkward position.

Meanwhile Louisa Caton, soon to be wife of Sir Felton Hervey Bathurst, the man who had captured Georgy's attentions in Brussels, together with her beautiful sisters was making quite the impression on London society. They were the granddaughters of the last surviving signatory of the American Declaration of Independence and were fabulously wealthy. Louisa, Marianne and Emily caused as much of a stir on London's social scene as the Lennox sisters had done in Brussels. These three beauties would add yet another challenge to those in competition for Wellington's affections. Marianne, the eldest, was already married to a Mr. Robert Patterson. Tall and slim with brunette hair, her confidence, charm and polish immediately attracted the attention of Wellington. He was transfixed by her and they began to be seen together regularly. Whether they had a sexual relationship has long been discussed and disputed. Wellington clearly felt very strongly for her as he commissioned a pair of portraits of himself and Marianne by the most famous portraitist of the day, Sir Thomas Lawrence. This is not something he had done before, even for his wife. Lawrence's beautiful portrayal of Marianne was then copied in miniature and secreted in a hidden compartment in one of the Duke's Breguet watches which he carried with him always. If each had not already been married, a proposal would surely have been made. Marianne was everything that a Duke required in a Duchess which sadly Wellington felt he did not receive from Kitty. We do not know Georgy's opinion of her, but it is likely there was a great feeling of rivalry and perhaps even resentment at Marianne's sudden accession to the Duke's most intimate confidante.

Louisa Caton had made a favourable first impression, as Freemantle reported: 'The Duke and all of us have been very busy ushering around Mrs Patterson and her sisters… I confess I have been very much epris [the prize] with the young one Miss Louisa Caton. There never was so naïve a little creature.'[153] Wellington was certainly under the Caton family's spell. In London Felton's marriage to Louisa was imminent. As Wellington now wrote 'I hope you make a greater impression in other quarters.'[154] Georgy retreated back into London society to escape the disappointment of Felton's decision to marry another woman. She was also realising that her relationship with the Duke would never be more than friendship and that her adoration of him was a distraction from meaningful relationships with other men; men with whom she had a real chance of happiness. The Duke in turn showed great sensitivity in dealing with Georgy's disillusionment in regard to her personal life, writing to support her in her courtships but at the same time imploring her to continue her friendship with him: 'I am delighted that you are going to England. I wish I could be there. I think we could contrive some amusement for ourselves...You will see all your Soupriants and Enemies in London; but I hope you will not forget me and that you will write to me sometimes.'[155] Georgy spent the rest of the summer in London, trying to get over her disappointments and finding suitable distractions amongst the many parties to be had there.

In October 1817 Georgy and her mother returned to Cambrai. Louisa Caton, now Lady Hervey, was already there and immediately there was tension between Louisa and the other English ladies. An imposter from a foreign country who had married one of their most eligible men was not welcome amongst their ranks. One evening, when they were playing a rousing game of 'Riding the Coach', the following incident occurred, in which Georgy had a part:

> 'you must know that a week ago, after several times having broached the subject, [that] she [Louisa] must ride in the rug, and said something amounting to the duke ordering the ADCs to draw her, upon which A[rthur] Hill said very stoutly that he would not. The rug was produced, the duchess (ours), Lady G Lennox, and Louisa were there, and upon asking who would ride, Louisa volunteered, but there was a general cry for the duchess first, Lady G Lennox hot in second. Louisa went away, but Felton went and fetched her. Four of the horses [the ADCs ordered to draw the ladies] went away immediately and she was left (with Campbell and Felton) to be drawn, when I saw what was happening I went to act as coachman, but no entreaties from our duchess could prevail on A Hill, G Lennox, or the rest to go and assist. She then came into the drawing room and told the duke, she had not

> had a coachman, upon which he immediately replied 'I'll be Coachman'; but she stammered & said she had no horse.'[156]

Freemantle continued 'Lady Georgina Lennox tells me, she told the duke, that she [Louisa] was not liked & that one and all had declared that they would not draw her.'[157] Louisa was understandably upset when the others ganged up on her and the Duke did his best to play down their dislike. Incredibly Freemantle wrote home that her nickname amongst the men was 'Chitty' but 'with an S.'[158] 'Riding the Coach' was further enlivened by the introduction of Lord Arthur Hill's mule, who had been trained to pull the rug with the lady perched on top. The mule drew Georgy 'to perfection, and Louisa was persuaded to try afterwards, she had no sooner seated herself, when said mule let fly such a volley as to make her and all the ladies take to their heels at a smart pace.'[159] No doubt a fair amount of unkind laughter was enjoyed at Louisa's expense. At dinner constant gibes were made against America and Louisa was driven away to bed in tears.

Freemantle recorded that 'The great amusements here are 1st rowing, and second talking tawdry to the Duchess of Richmond, who enjoys it extremely.'[160] The Duchess's nickname was 'Old Mother Richmond'. Two new plays were in preparation and all were busy preparing their parts. A 'Love Box' had been set up in which everyone contributed a witty epitaph in a feigned hand, which was then read out for entertainment. Freemantle reported home: 'No words can convey to you a just idea of the scenes of gambols going on here. Old Richmond is pinched black and blue all over, and Lady Georgina [sic] is beset by Percy & Cathcart, having young Uxbridge & Charles Fitzroy as cats paws.'[161] Once again Georgy was proving to be the life and soul of the party. Now playing four of Wellington's staff officers off against each other she was certainly moving on from her disappointments over Felton and Hotham. As Christmas drew near, the parties, plays and other entertainments continued apace. The Duke of Richmond, along with Mary and Jane, arrived to join the parties and to enjoy the festive season en famille.

Unfortunately Lady Charlotte Greville also arrived in Cambrai around this time. It was well known that the two families were at 'daggers drawn with each other.'[162] Freemantle wrote, 'it is consequently great fun to watch the different feelings of envy and jealousy of Old Richmond at the attention paid to Lady Charlotte in preference to her daughters.'[163] Lady Charlotte, Wellington's great love from the time of the Battle of Waterloo, had come to hold court once more. The Duchess of Richmond was not however going to let her young and vivacious daughters be outshone by Lady Charlotte. Wellington's staff officers approved of the elegant and refined Lady Charlotte, as 'the Duke is always in good spirits when she is with him',[164] although 'Old Mother Richmond' remained their firm favourite.

Georgy leaves a rather convenient gap in her writings after she and her parents leave Cambrai early in 1818. Until her marriage in 1824 she gives very few details about her day to day life. A certain amount of deduction and guesswork can be made but the truth as to why she did not marry until that time will always be a mystery. The years following the Battle of Waterloo had been some of the most raucous and fun of her life. Georgy had failed to make fast her affections to one man although several had caught her eye. There was also the added problem of her lack of fortune. Any serious suitor needed to be rich enough to support Georgy to the satisfaction of the Lennox family. Her courtships with Felton, Hotham, and Rous had been formative experiences. Furthermore, she was still besotted with the Duke who she idolised above all other men. Over the next few years Georgy lived mostly in London. Her adventures during this part of her life are largely untold, which leaves us with the tantalizing task of unravelling her story from the few facts which we know.

CHAPTER SIX

Tragedies & Love Affairs

'The Duke looked over my shoulder as I read the account, and as my tears fell on the paper I perceived that he was also much affected.'[165]

Lady Shelley, on the Duke of Wellington's response when told about the death of the Duke of Richmond

In London there was a new feeling of optimism after many years of war with the French. Memorials to Wellington and the Battle of Waterloo were springing up in the form of monuments, renamed streets and even in the form of a bridge across the Thames which was opened to great acclaim in 1817. Wellington, although rarely in London during this period, was still the name on everybody's lips.

The most famous man of his generation, his presence at a party would send visible vibrations through the room as every head turned to catch a glimpse of their hero. Georgy continued to bask in the light of his stardom whenever they were together. In her eyes, he was the ultimate hero.

It was the beginning of 1818 when Georgy and her siblings returned permanently to England. Witnessing Waterloo and the antics that followed at Cambrai were experiences that coloured and shaped their lives. Life back in England took on a familiar jaunt of visits, dinners and parties. Invitations flowed in from all corners of the city and beyond. It was time for Georgy to marry and settle but a tragedy soon befell the family which pushed all thoughts of marriage to the back of her mind.

The Richmond family were to be split once more when the Duke of Richmond received news of his next posting. He was to be sent to Canada as the next Governor-in-Chief of British North America. The voyage would be perilous and Canada, when reached, was known to be a dangerous place, with wild expanses of uncharted land to travel through. It was not a job to be undertaken lightly and the news was met with sadness from the whole family. There was no talk of a return date, indeed it was unclear whether the Duke would ever return. Affairs had to be put in order, so Richmond had a general power of attorney drawn up which gave powers to Wellington, March and Lord Bathurst in his absence, with the document still in the Goodwood archive today. It was decided that four of his daughters, Mary, Louisa, Charlotte and Sophia would accompany him to Canada. Maitland, Sarah's husband, had been appointed Governor of Upper Canada and so he too would relocate with the group.

Georgy and the rest of her siblings remained behind, housed amongst willing relations. Young Arthur Lennox was informally adopted by the Duchess of Wellington and spent his school holidays at Stratfield Saye, the country estate in Hampshire which Wellington had purchased after Waterloo. The Duchess of Richmond was left in charge of the younger children whilst March and his wife moved into Molecomb, where Georgy had spent her earliest years. It seemed natural that Georgy should live with Lord and Lady Bathurst at Cirencester House. Georgy adored Lady Bathurst and the feeling was warmly reciprocated. Lady Bathurst, sister of Georgy's father, had always taken an active interest in her young niece's welfare and was delighted to welcome her into their home. Georgy was also close with the Bathurst children, especially Seymour Bathurst and Lady Georgina Bathurst.

Moving away from his homeland once again was another sacrifice for Richmond but the financial necessity to work and support his family was still paramount as the family debt remained high. His relationship with his wife continued to be stormy and it was known in London that the Duchess was still gambling heavily. Amongst others she reportedly owed Blücher, whose Prussian troops had bolstered Wellington's in his hour of need at Waterloo, the colossal sum of £30,000.[166] The family would have to rely on the small income earned by the Duke and any potential good marriages made by the Lennox daughters. Until some major financial relief came to their rescue Richmond would have to endure life as an expatriate. The party reached Quebec around a month after leaving England. Despite the dangers, the position was an exciting opportunity for Georgy's father and he embarked on the new adventure with his characteristic enthusiasm and joie de vivre.

The Duke of Richmond was accompanied on his daily excursions by

Captain William Bowles, a charming and loyal Naval Officer. A party including both men had set out shortly after their arrival, on a reconnaissance of Quebec and Lower Canada. It was whilst out on one of these surveying trips that Richmond was bitten by a stray rabid fox. Louisa recalled 'my Father came into our Room with a Handkerchief over his Hand saying that a Nasty little Fox had attacked Blucher a pet spaniel always with my father and he had saved Blucher but the Fox had bitten his hand.'[167] The fox bite became infected and it began to affect his mind in the way that only the much-feared disease hydrophobia could. More commonly called rabies, this disease was at the time extremely rare, there was no cure and it was often fatal. An account of his slow and painful death was given to Lady Shelley, a mutual friend of the Wellington and Richmond families:

> 'Nothing can exceed the magnamity and fortitude displayed by the Duke from the moment he was aware of the nature of his malady. He well knew that there was no hope of a cure, or even delay its fatal termination; but he carefully concealed this from those who were with him. The Duke proceeded on his journey with increasing spasms in his throat and shoulder. While walking through a swamp, Major Bowles, who was close to him, stepped into some water and made a slight splash. The Duke sprang aside quickly, and exclaimed: 'Bowles, what can your treading in water have with my shoulder? Yet it gave me a dreadful spasm.' On reaching a ravine his spasms increased, and the party experienced so much difficulty in getting the Duke to cross it that they feared a brain fever was coming on. They never once suspected the real cause. On coming up to the boat the Duke asked if there was no other possible way to get down. He appeared to be much agitated, and very reluctant to enter the boat. At last he said 'Tie a hankerchief over my eyes, and lead me to the boat, for I cannot get into it by myself.' This was done, and the

> Duke threw himself flat on his face and clutched the sides of the boat. As the boat was pushed off Major Bourke's suspicions were aroused, and he whispered to Colonel Cockburn that it must be a case of hydrophobia! Before they had proceeded twenty yards the splashing of the water disturbed the oars, causing the Duke violent agitation. He kept on crying out: 'Take me on shore instantly, or I shall die!' They put back at once; and the moment the Duke set foot on land, he broke away from them and fled through the woods- leaping over fences and other obstacles with all the agility and strength of a hunted animal flying for its life!'

The Duke's attendants were in great distress and followed as quickly as they could. At last they caught sight of him flying through the undergrowth before them like a madman without his hat and covered in mud. With great difficulty they caught up with him and saw him enter a barn and throw himself upon some straw. He cried out: 'Here Charles Lennox meets his fate!'"[168]

He was not wrong. Over the torturous hours that followed, the Duke slipped in and out of sanity, in acute pain. As night fell he 'fancied himself with the Duke of Wellington in battle; he cheered on his men, rallied them, etc, with all the fire and impetuosity of a hero bent on victory. He then seemed to think that he was fighting in defence of Quebec; and he had been wounded, and was dying. He expressed a wish to buried under the ramparts.'[169] In moments of lucidity, the Duke dictated a long letter of farewell to his family with individual messages for each member. This would become a cherished letter for Georgy and her sisters. In part he dictated:

> 'Tell March that I know he will regret being D of Richmond but that I am satisfied I leave my Titles & Estates to one of

> the most honourable men in England. Tell him I know he will take care of his mother and sisters...Love to dear little Georgy, I leave Harriet & Emma [two of their dogs] to her... Remember me to the Duke of Wellington...Tell Sarah that with my last words I forgive her & Genl Maitland from the bottom of my soul & they & their family have my blessing.'[170]

Captain Bowles reported what happened next, in an account still in the de Ros archive:

> 'He could not lay down; but walked about slowly, holding my arm...He was perfectly convinced that he could not recover and dictated messages and remembrances to his family and friends, and excepting during one or two violent attacks of spasms, he was perfectly quiet...the Duke consented to be blooded, and about two pints were taken from his arm, this appeared at first to relieve him, but the paroxysms soon returned and became more violent every moment. During the intervals he was perfectly sensible and his thoughts invariably reverted to his family and his friends. Towards evening he was able to swallow about twenty drops of laudanum and afterwards took a grain of solid opium in a little chicken broth, of which he swallowed a few spoonfulls two or three times. His kind and affectionate manner never forsook him for a moment, and he knew those about him till nearly midnight- about sunset we removed him into the farm house which was prepared for his reception. He was still sufficiently strong to walk with assistance from the barn into the house, where he laid down on the bed- from that time he evidently grew weaker every hour and his mind wandered more constantly. Towards midnight he fell into a sort of stupor and from that period appeared to have ceased suffering. About Eight in the morning of the twenty Eight he expired without the slightest struggle.'[171]

Bowles was greatly moved by the event and indeed his kind recollections of the Duke's bravery and fortitude in the face of death proved a great consolation to the family. Georgy kept Bowles' account of the Duke's last days for the rest of her life. Richmond's broken body was taken back to Quebec with the greatest solemnity and he was buried in the Cathedral of the Holy Trinity. It was Lady Shelley who broke the news to the Duke of Wellington and they both wept. The Duke wrote to Georgy after a suitable amount of time had elapsed:

> 'I have not written to you since the accounts were received of the dreadful misfortune which has occurred; but I am sure you will give me credit for having felt it and for you as I ought; and for the motives of my silence. I am anxious however to have a line from you to tell me how you are; as well as to have some account of the Duchess and Jane. Pray remember me to them most kindly. You will have heard that I am to have the charge of Arthur [Georgy's younger brother]. Will you ask the Duchess whether she approves of what I propose to do for him, or whether she wishes to have him educated for any other line or profession. I will do anything that his friends approve of. I propose that of Woolwich [through his position as Master-General of the Ordnance] as being immediately under my own hand. God bless you dearest Georgy.'[172]

Wellington continued to do all he could for the Lennox family including securing a commission for young Sussex Lennox. He now felt a sense of responsibility to care for the Richmond children after the loss of their father, despite his own busy schedule. The year before Richmond's death Wellington had been made Master-General of the Ordnance under the Premiership of Lord Liverpool. It was a position he held until 1827 when he resigned to become Prime Minister. Having always taken an active interest in the governing of the country he had saved from the clutches of Napoleon, he became an increasingly influential member of the Tory party. Whether Georgy replied to his kind letter, we do not know, as nothing from her side of her correspondence with Wellington has survived. Indeed, the story of Georgy's life is almost entirely muted during this sad time. It appears from a letter in the de Ros archive that Georgy, reunited with her sisters who had returned to England after the Duke's funeral, was residing at Culford, home to the Earls of Cardigan. After her initial distress her aunt wrote that Georgy was now 'more calm', focusing her attentions on caring for her distraught mother. Lady Bathurst wrote the following:

> 'I cannot resist my beloved Georgy writing you a very few lines- I will not attempt to express all we have & our suffering...& for all you & poor Jane have been through! You are getting a little more calm & this at present is all we can expect to hear. Rest assured my Dearest we shall always be too happy to have you & that you will ever find with us a home- at present I hope you will stay at Culford. I think it is better for you all.'[173]

At Culford the next few weeks were spent in quiet mourning. The Duchess had taken the news of her husband's death very badly and the two sisters did all they could to comfort her. Georgy in turn was comforted by letters which reflected the love felt for both her father and the rest of the family: 'by & by when yr mind is more composed it will be gratifying to you to hear the universal, the public as well as private regrets, of every creature both at home & abroad- we are overwhelmed with letters of anxious expression after you.'[174] After leaving Culford Georgy moved permanently into Cirencester House, where she felt most at home.

The death of the Duke of Richmond was a catalyst for change and not only marked the end of Georgy's childhood but effectively brought about the break-up of the Richmond family. March became the 5th Duke of Richmond and moved into Goodwood. Although popular as Lord March, some doubted his suitability for the role as head of one of the most important Ducal families in the country: 'as to the Duke of Richmond, he has not brains enough to fill the smallest thimble that ever fitted the smallest lady's finger,'[175] was one rather unkind comment.

With time, Georgy's grief subsided and she began to engage once again in the delights of London society. She enjoyed meeting the friends of her aunt and uncle and as Lord Bathurst was at this time a member of the Liverpool administration, Georgy was thrown into London's thrilling political society. As the months passed Georgy's sparkle returned. She was certainly still beautiful despite her recent sufferings and health problems. She was later described at this time as being of 'small stature, but very well-proportioned, with beautifully formed hands and feet. Her features were regular, with a delicate and transparent complexion.'[176] She was a natural beauty with grace and charm to match her quick wit and ready laugh. Now free from the controlling glare of her mother from across the dining room table, Georgy was able to socialise with more freedom and intent.

One day Georgy was taken to visit her great aunt, the infamous Lady Sarah Napier of Holland House. Before her marriage she had been the other Lady Sarah Lennox, one of the glamourous and wild daughters of the 2nd Duke of Richmond. This was the same entrancing Sarah Lennox whose name had so upset King George III when he was introduced to her great-niece all those years later; feeling the contours of a

4. Hand painted illumination by Georgiana, Lady de Ros.
Based on The Book of Hours, a devotional manuscript from the Middle Ages

5. A miniature of Georgy's mother, Charlotte Lennox, 4th Duchess of Richmond.

6. Georgy's father, Lord Charles Lennox, later 4th Duke of Richmond, by Henry Collen after John Hoppner, 1823. © The Trustees of the Goodwood Collection

7 Sir Arthur Wellesley, 1804–5, by Robert Home. A three quarter length version of the original full length, which is in the Royal Collection. This version is owned by the Wellington Family and hangs at Apsley House.

8. A portrait miniature traditionally known as Lady Georgiana Lennox, who was always called Georgy by her friends.

9. A portrait miniature of Sir Arthur Wellesley, by Richard Cosway R.A, 1808.

10. A miniature of the 1st Duke of Wellington, 1815.
This is the miniature given to Lady Georgiana Lennox on the eve of the Battle of Waterloo. On the back is inscribed in Georgy's handwriting 'This miniature is an original and was given to me by the Duke of Wellington at Brussels on 15 June 1815 [signed] 'Georgiana de Ros'.
This miniature is now in a private collection in New York. A copy is in the de Ros family collection.

11. A watercolour of the site of Lord Hay's burial at Waterloo, painted by Georgy after her marriage.

12. The Duchess of Richmond's Ball on the 15th June 1815, by Robert Alexander Hillingsford.

13. Part of the silver service given to Lady Georgiana de Ros by the 1st Duke of Wellington on the occasion of her marriage in 1824.

14. 1st Duke of Wellington, a miniature on enamel by William Essex, after Sir Thomas Lawrence, 1838

15. A miniature of Lady Georgiana de Ros, 1832

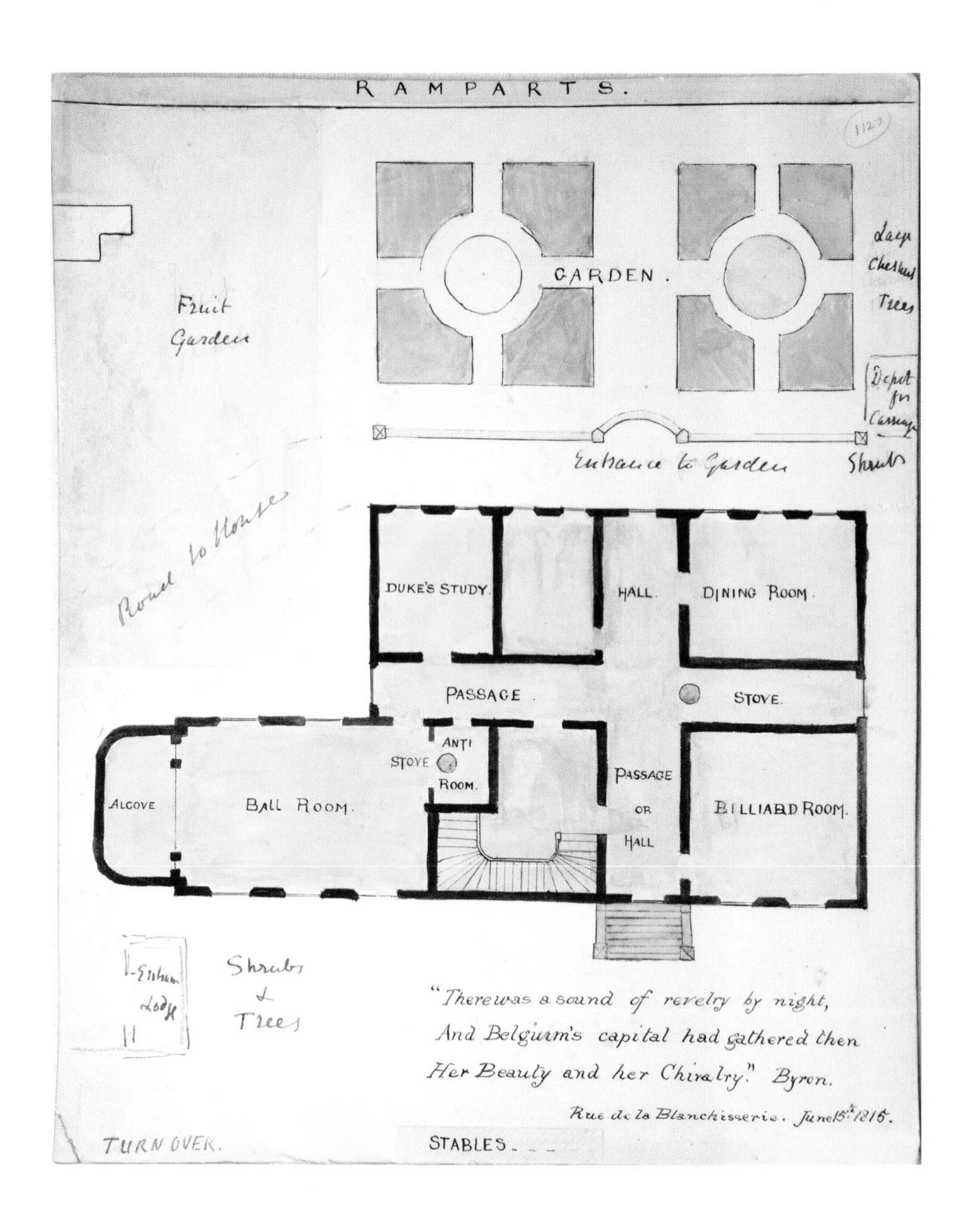

16. A hand annotated drawing by Georgy and her siblings, showing the exact location of their mother's ball on 15th June 1815.

17. A photograph taken by Dudley of (left-right) Dudley's wife Georgiana, Lady de Ros, and the Hon. Blanche de Ros, 1858. Acquired by Queen Victoria. Royal Collection Trust/© Her Majesty Queen Elizabeth II 2016

18. A portrait of Georgy by her mother-in-law, Charlotte, Lady de Ros

19. Dudley Fitzgerald-de Ros as a young boy, 1840

20. William Fitzgerald-de Ros, c.1840

21. **Georgy in later years, a chalk sketch by Countess Feodora Gleichen, 1871**

22. Dudley when 24th Baron de Ros, in his 'Spy' Vanity Fair portrait, entitled 'The Premier Baron'.

23. Large miniature on ivory by Robert Thorburn of the 1st Duke of Wellington with four of his grandchildren in the library at Stratfield Saye, 1852. This portrait was commissioned by Angela Burdett-Coutts and is now in the Wellington family collection.
© Stratfield Saye Preservation Trust

24. The family vault at the chapel at Old Court, Strangford, where Georgy and William are buried. © Paul Flanagan.

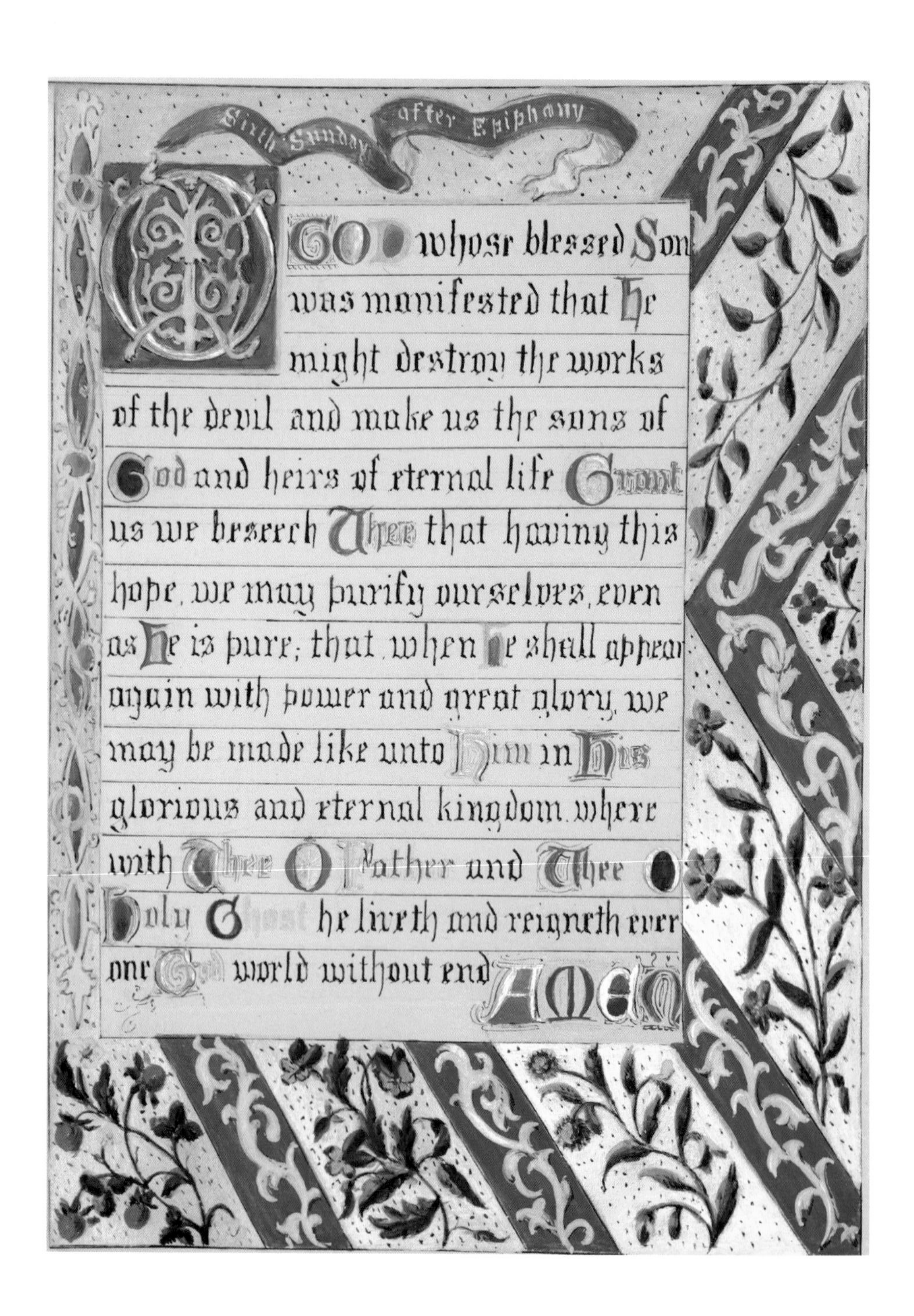

25. Another religious illumination by Georgiana, Lady de Ros

face similar to the one he had loved so long ago. Sarah had ended up making a bad marriage to a man called Charles Bunbury, which had led to infamy, gambling and adultery on both sides. After bearing an illegitimate child with her lover Lord William Gordon, Sarah bravely divorced Bunbury, and finally found happiness in the arms of the Hon. George Napier. The couple married in 1781 and went on to have eight children. Having grown up hearing stories about the infamous Lennox sisters who shared her name and heritage, it was exciting for Georgy to meet her notorious relative. Now blind, Sarah Napier had borne several successful sons, in particular Sir George Napier, who famously fought under Campbell and Wellington and lost an arm at the storming of Ciudad Rodrigo.

Georgy's reputation would never reach the heights of her wild great aunt Lady Sarah Napier, yet her own behaviour at this time did begin to attract the attention of the London gossips. Her love of socialising had been acceptable whilst she had been younger at Brussels, and in the heady atmosphere of victorious Cambrai. The Duchess had tolerated Georgy's flirtations and her father had always kept a close eye on his beautiful daughters, almost always managing to keep them in line. With the 4th Duke of Richmond gone and her mother distracted with her own social life, Georgy was allowed more freedom whilst she lived under the Bathursts' roof. She now could decide what kind of life she was going to carve out for herself. Was she to lead a life like her great aunt Sarah, or follow her siblings into respectable marriages? As the months slipped away, Georgy grappled with the expectations she had for herself, as well as those of her family.

With Georgy now living in London and Wellington spending much of his time between town and Stratfield Saye, long gossipy letters were no longer needed. News and scandal could be discussed in person. However, it is curious when studying the body of letters so carefully preserved by Georgy that none from October 1818 to August 1820 survives, especially as Wellington's last letter to her, on the death of her father, was so intimate. As one of Richmond's closest friends and contemporaries, Wellington was the perfect substitute for a father's love and had always been keen to maintain written links between them. The thought that they did not correspond at all over these years is highly unlikely, so the reason for the gap in the archive could be that the letters were considered by Georgy, or her daughter Blanche, to be too intimate to keep. The Duke normally destroyed all personal correspondence throughout his lifetime, and was careful to ensure that no trace of Georgy's letters to him survived after his death. His passion for privacy was well known and from the flirtatious letters that do survive between them, the Duke's reasons to suppress them are obvious.

Whatever the status of Georgy's relationship with the Duke she was certainly enjoying a lot of male attention at this time. The celebrated diarist Charles Greville was one such conquest. Greville was closely connected to many of Georgy's friends and relations and we know that they had known each other before Georgy had moved to Brussels because she mentions him in one of her letters to Lady Bathurst. Several years after his death Greville's diaries were published containing damning accounts of his contemporaries' characters and various insalubrious dramas. They remain a well-known source for scandalous details about celebrities of the time. Although Greville rarely commented on his personal life, he did write the following entry on 16th July 1822:

'Since I last wrote I have been continuously in town...and I

> have done nothing but make love to Georgina [sic] Lennox. At the Priory I went to her room at night but was fool enough to go away without doing anything. I shall not be such a fool again…I have been very often bored to death by the necessity of paying some attention to keep up an interest with G.L. Having had so much trouble, I don't choose to drop it without bringing the thing to a conclusion.'[177]

'Bringing the thing to a conclusion' could have referred to Georgy's virginity, as it is not likely to have been a marriage proposal given Greville's incredible reputation for womanising and home-wrecking. Whether this was ever 'concluded' is not recorded in any future diary entry and Georgy herself leaves little record of her relationship with Greville behind. Indeed, the affair was short lived, lasting only for the summer of 1822. Although lust was undoubtedly Greville's main reason for pursuing Georgy so intently, he was also well-known for bearing a grudge against Wellington as his mother, Lady Charlotte Greville, had been one of the Duke's most respected mistresses. Greville took this as a personal slight, and could have conducted the affair to get back at Wellington by taking one of his closest female friends away from him. If he had managed to secure a marriage to Georgy, quite a social coup for himself, this would have greatly displeased Wellington. Georgy certainly would not have told Wellington about her relationship with Greville as she knew that they greatly disliked each other. If Wellington had known about the affair he surely would have been appalled at the news that was to come, which was to put a definitive end to the short-lived affair between Georgy and Greville. A short while later it was discovered that another of Greville's conquests, the wife of Sir Bellingham Graham, was pregnant with his child. Georgy now knew for sure that this dishonourable scoundrel was not the man for her, but it had been another less than satisfactory love-match which left her feeling disheartened.

CHAPTER SEVEN

Boyle Farm

'Miss Boyle, I heard last night had consented to marry Lord Henry Fitzgerald. I think they have chosen well'[178]

Horace Walpole on the intended marriage of Miss Charlotte Boyle to Lord Henry Fitzgerald

Greville had many male friends who were well known for their excessive gambling, drinking and casual use of prostitutes. Their names were often alluded to in the papers and they were regularly seen leaving London's most prestigious clubs, bleary-eyed, at unusual times of day. Two such friends were brothers Henry Fitzgerald- de Ros (who inherited the title of Lord de Ros in 1829) and his younger brother William. In time the brothers were introduced to Georgy and her sisters. As her dalliance with Greville came to an end, Georgy and William Fitzgerald- de Ros were found increasingly in each other's company.

We do not know exactly when Georgy was introduced to William but it was certainly not long before they were falling in love. William was kind, attentive and handsome, and both felt increasingly comfortable with each other. Georgy was now twenty-nine years old and considered an old bride. William was only a Lieutenant in the Army and as such had limited resources with which to support her. Despite being the daughter of a Duke, Georgy was seen to be making the better match. Lacking financial resources and nearing her thirties, Georgy was no longer the young catch she had been when she had returned from Brussels. From the start, it was not a love- match that suited both families. Although from a good family William was not the eldest son and it was Henry who would inherit all the de Ros title and estates. In this respect William and Georgy's social positions were not dissimilar. Although Georgy came from a higher social pedigree, any money was tied up in the estates which had passed onto her brother, now 5th Duke of Richmond, leaving Georgy with nothing.

The history of the de Ros family is in itself a fascinating subject. Its long and complex history can at times be a little baffling. The de Ros title (at times spelt de Roose and always pronounced with a long 'o' sound) is one of the most ancient baronial titles in Britain's peerage, tracing its lineage back to the year 1264. Two thirteenth-century de Ros knights can been seen entombed in the Temple church in London and at Bottesford in Leicestershire respectively. Fast forward seven hundred and fifty years, the current Baron is the 28th incumbent and still lives on the de Ros estate in Northern Ireland. He is the Premier Baron of England as he holds the title with the longest existing line. Unlike most titles which can only be passed through the male line, the de Ros title can be passed to daughters if there is no male heir.

Indeed, this has been done on six separate occasions in the title's history, an unusual and impressive feat. With this type of inheritance it is not necessarily the eldest daughter who can claim the title if there is more than one daughter in line to inherit. Due to this complication the barony has fallen into abeyance on more than one occasion. Each time it has been brought back by petitioning the monarch, and each claimant has been a strong-minded and lineage proud de Ros woman; again most unusual.

The title was held by the de Ros family until the early 16th century when it merged with that of the Earl of Rutland. The title remained with members of the Rutland family until it was inherited by the 6th Earl's daughter, who married the 1st Duke of Buckingham. The Duke was famously, and scandalously, the lover of King James I. Buckingham's son George inherited both the barony and the dukedom but upon his death in 1687 both titles became dormant. Over a century later in 1790, William's grandmother, Mrs Charlotte Boyle-Walsingham, petitioned George III to terminate the abeyance of the barony in her favour. Her claim to the title was tenuous to say the least. She was distantly related to the younger brother of the 15th Baron de Ros but she considered the title her birth right. With it would come higher social position and privileges, something Charlotte was keen to fight for. After long deliberations, her request was refused and Charlotte was forced to let the matter lie for the moment. She now turned her attention to another personal project, that of her house in Thames Ditton, near London. This house would become the scene of many a party and William and Georgy would later spend many happy months there.

Charlotte was independently wealthy having been the sole beneficiary of her father's will. Having chosen as her husband the Hon. Robert

Boyle Walsingham, a son of the Earl of Shannon, Charlotte purchased the estate in Thames Ditton from Lord Hertford in 1784. Many of her family would end up living in the house or on the estate over the years to come. Charlotte had the old house demolished and built again from scratch, naming it 'Boyle Farm'. Soon it had 'pleasure grounds, orchards, gardens, fields, lawns, shrubberies, greenhouse, farmyards, barns, stables, etc. and boathouse close, and various parcels of land.'[179] It was a pastoral idyll and yet still a comfortable distance from London. The estate included several islands on the river and the house had stunning views of the park at Hampton Court. By design the house was not overly grand or imposing. Horace Walpole, who was a good friend, wrote that: 'Mrs Walsingham is making her house at Ditton, now baptised Boyle Farm, very orthodox.'[180] Visitors included not only Walpole but the greatest portraitist of the age Sir Joshua Reynolds and the famous diarist Fanny Burney. Charlotte was an accomplished painter herself and decorated much of the interiors. Some of her engravings are today in the collection of the British Museum. Fanny Burney had this to say of the decorations in the house:

> 'They appear to me surprisingly well executed, and the subjects are admirably chosen and selected. They are chiefly copies from old pictures, or from Sir Joshua Reynolds. She has also copied Gainsborough's sweet Shepherd's Boy; and there are originals, by herself, of Capt. Dalsingham, and her son, and Miss Boyle. These are all in oils. There are also some heads in Crayon, and several small figures in Plaster of paris by Miss Boyle, who inherits her mother's genius and fondness for painting.'[181]

The Miss Boyle mentioned here was Charlotte's daughter and William's mother. Charlotte entertained on a lavish scale in town and at Boyle Farm. The lawn sloping down to the Thames was often filled with lights and elegantly dressed guests being entertained late into the night. Their hostess was strong-headed, she 'took care to invite no company to her house whom she disposed to disdain.'[182] She was in many ways similar in character to the Dowager Duchess of Richmond, being 'only civil to people of birth, fame or wealth, and extremely insolent to all others.'[183] Two of the attendees of a lavish ball held there in 1788 were Wellington's mother Lady Mornington and her daughters Lady Mary and Anne Wellesley. After Charlotte's death the house was left to her only daughter Charlotte Boyle, who continued improvements to the house. She also took up the mantle of fighting for the family's claim to the de Ros barony. Being her mother's sole beneficiary and inheriting a fortune to the tune of £200,000, Charlotte was one of the wealthiest heiress's in England at the age of just twenty-one years old. She proved to be just as strong willed as her mother and did not intend to let the matter of the de Ros barony rest for long.

In August 1791 Charlotte married Lord Henry Fitzgerald, a son of the 1st Duke of Leinster, whilst his mother the Duchess of Leinster had once been Lady Emily Lennox; sister of the 3rd Duke of Richmond. The ceremony took place at the Boyle-Walsingham's London home and one of the witnesses was Georgy's father the Duke of Richmond. Nine years senior to his new wife, Henry had been educated at Eton, after which he had joined the Army and served in the West Indies, quickly rising to the rank of Lieutenant-Colonel. He was a highly regarded amateur thespian who delighted society at every party he attended. The young married couple quickly settled down to life at Boyle Farm.

Henry's parents, the Duke and Duchess of Leinster, had twenty children together, an incredible number even by the standards of the time. Such amazing reproductive ability did not hamper the Duchess's health or good looks and soon after the death of her husband she married the children's tutor, which delighted her children as they regarded Mr. Ogilvie as more of a father than the Duke had been. The Duchess enjoyed long stays at Boyle Farm as Charlotte and Henry began to add to their own family. In all, twelve children came of this happy union and eight of those were born at Thames Ditton. They were all baptised at the nearby church of St. Nicholas. The Duchess of Leinster was visited at Boyle Farm by her sister Lady Sarah Napier, who wrote that 'I passed a day with my sister Leinster at Boyle Farm, which is now the seat of luxury, & beauty, & ingenuity, it would have taken me a week to see all the fine things in the house.'[184] The Duchess of Leinster continued to enjoy the beautiful surroundings at Boyle Farm in the company of her extended family until her death at the age of eighty-three.

One of the Duchess's twenty children was the extraordinarily popular Irish revolutionary Lord Edward Fitzgerald, father to Georgy's good friend Pamela Fitzgerald. The whole Fitzgerald family had been thrown into a deep despair by the death of their beloved Lord Edward. His mother recovered from her loss by retreating to the quiet serenity of Boyle Farm. The Duchess's daughter-in-law Charlotte Boyle was however much less sympathetic and would not allow Edward's widow Lady Pamela to come to Thames Ditton. This was perhaps because Charlotte was in the throes of getting the de Ros barony called out of abeyance and she did not want the family name dragged into Irish republican politics. In 1806 she finally succeeded in convincing the

Committee of Privileges to accept her application for the Barony of de Ros. Her case was supported by her friend the Prime Minister Lord Grenville who wrote a personal letter to George III asking 'Whether your Majesty would be graciously pleased to determine the abeyance of the Barony of Roos in favour of Lady Henry Fitzgerald, which, if your Majesty had no objection to it, Lord Grenville would venture to recommend.'[185] The King himself replied 'Lady Henry Fitzgerald having been at so much expense and trouble in regard to the Barony of Roos, and having brought forward the case so clearly, the king considers it very fair to grant the abeyance in her favour, as recommended by Lord Grenville.'[186] She became the twenty-first Baroness de Ros in her own right, changing the family name to Fitzgerald-de Ros and was thereafter called Lady de Ros. The same year Henry was appointed Ireland's Post-Master General, proving that Charlotte's efforts were already proving beneficial to the fortunes of the family.

Life at Boyle Farm continued in a tranquil way punctuated by splendid gatherings which brought together Henry and Charlotte's friends and acquaintances, many of the most famous names of the day among them. It was around this time that Henry also began an affair with Princess Caroline of Brunswick, the estranged wife of the Prince of Wales. Tied to a hapless marriage which had been undertaken to appease Parliament and relieve the Prince Regent of some of his debts, Caroline was hated and distrusted by most of the establishment but loved by the people. Henry was often to be seen riding out with Caroline or sitting in her box at the theatre. In the end it was Henry's wife, now Lady de Ros, who put an end to the affair. Since Lady de Ros held the purse strings, it was easy for her to control her husband when he made the mistake of straying from her side. She made her husband write a letter to Caroline, stating that 'from motives of friendship towards her, he conceived it his duty to relinquish the honour of being so frequently in her Royal Highness's society.'[187]

Despite this, Henry was still invited to many of the Princess's functions. Her lady-in-waiting wrote: '...Lord Henry Fitzgerald dined at Kensington. It is comical to see how the Princess behaves to him, trying to show off, and yet endeavouring to make him hate her. His behaviour is perfectly kind, respectful, and even at times there is a sadness in his manner, which makes me think he regrets the change in her sentiments towards him; and I am certain he is sorry to see the alteration there is in the society which frequents her Royal Highness's house.'[188] Henry continued to see the Princess socially until 1814, when she was forced to live abroad. She returned to England when her husband became George IV, but was turned away from the coronation service; hated as she was by the King's establishment.

Summers for the de Ros family were spent at their country estate in Strangford, Northern Ireland. The estate had been endowed to Lord Henry Fitzgerald by his older brother the 2nd Duke of Leinster. The estate amounted to 3000 acres of land in County Down, with almost the same amount again in County Meath. The village of Strangford comprised of a commanding stretch of land running alongside the Irish sea with a picturesque village and harbour. Breath-taking views of the sea can still be viewed all the way along Fitzgerald land. The history of the place itself is enthralling. In 432AD, it was said that St. Patrick sailed up the Strangford narrows bringing Christianity with him to the pagan villagers who had made their home on the banks of the lough. This encouraged several monastic communities to flourish in the area. In turn Strangford witnessed the arrival of the

Vikings and then the Normans and soon became a blossoming trading region, being of important strategic positioning for those importing and exporting goods. Boat building, fishing and the production of kelp were important industries and helped to gentrify the area. In the sixteenth century castles were constructed in Strangford, Ward and Portaferry. The charming and unique family chapel on the de Ros estate at Strangford was built in 1629. It has been the resting place for members of the family ever since.

Charlotte and Henry's son William was born in 1797. As a young boy William always loved the beauty of Strangford and spent hours playing on the banks of the lough there. After Eton he joined the Life Guards. He was close to all of his many siblings, having five brothers and six sisters, although one brother and one sister did not survive infancy. He was especially close to his brother Arthur, who was the next eldest above him. William was the most conscientious and hardworking of the sons but the barony was still to be inherited by his eldest brother Henry, who was quite his opposite in character. Whereas William was steady and reliable, Henry had a rakish reputation for drinking and gambling. He was known to frequent houses of dubious repute, and gathered around him a gang of similarly minded friends. He was known as 'The Sarpent', or serpent, and one of his closest friends was Georgy's ex-lover Charles Greville. A rather extraordinary announcement in Greville's diary recorded that:

> 'I have been living at Fulham at Lord Wharncliffe's villa for six or seven weeks, keeping a girl [a prostitute] of whom, although she has good looks, good manners and is not ill-disposed, I am getting tired [of her] and doubt if ever I shall take one to live with me again. Henry de Ros who is the grand purveyor of women to all his friends, gave her to me; I have

> lived here in idleness and luxury giving dinners and wasting money rather more than usual.'[189]

So it appears that as well as his dissipation for fast living and bad choices, Henry was also a high class pimp for his friends. Despite their differences however, William and Henry had a good relationship. It was Henry's antics that had brought the de Ros family to the attention of London's gossips but he still remained an integral part of the de Ros family and life at Boyle Farm in particular. Handsome and charming, it was hoped that he would eventually settle down and make a happy marriage, a fate that now awaited his favourite little brother.

CHAPTER EIGHT

Contentment

'What an odd marriage William de Ros's is! Such an odd match for the girl, matchmaking and manoeuvring in the days of her youth going off in romance at eight and twenty.'[189a]

Lady Pamela Campbell, (neé Fitzgerald) to Miss Emily Eden

Georgy and William became engaged and knowing the decision was likely to be unpopular with both families, decided to revel in the secret of their agreement for a short time. A few close friends were told and so of course the news was soon known by more people than they would have liked. When the news of their engagement was finally broken to their respective families there was a decidedly mixed reaction. William recorded in his diary that he 'suddenly took courage at dinner & we told G&E [Lady Bathurst and her daughter Emily] in the Evening. They told Milady [the Duchess of Richmond] &

every thing was settled to make me happier than I had ever been. The contrary Lady de Ros was also told.'[190] Two days later William rode to Thames Ditton to tell his father who was 'all kindness & everyone doing their best for us.'[191] Both families agreed to the match but not without reservations and it was the two matriarchs, Lady de Ros and the Dowager Duchess of Richmond, who voiced the most discontent. This was probably because they understood how society would react to the union. In addition, Lady de Ros had heard tales of Georgy's wild reputation and despite her pedigree, did not believe her to be a catch for her beloved son. Georgy was now twenty-nine years old and considered quite old to be getting married and beginning a family. William was also only at the start of his military career. It was clear that it was going to be a financial struggle to maintain Georgy and any children they might have to the standard that their social class dictated.

No direct comments from the Lennox family survive, but Georgy's mother had a particularly good reason to disapprove of the de Ros family as that year news broke in society that Henry de Ros had fathered an illegitimate child with the daughter of a Mr William Spencer. The lady had then gone on to marry and become Countess Westerholt. The story is recounted in the diary of Wellington's close friend Harriet Arbuthnot after she and her husband attended a ball given by the Duke of Devonshire:

> 'before her marriage, [the Countess] had a child by Henry de Ros, son of Ld Henry Fitzgerald. This of course, being publicly known, drove her out of society in England & she went abroad & there married this German count. The family say the Count was informed of the circumstances of her former intrigue, & disregarded it till after the marriage he

> heard that her shame had been publicly known in England. Her father, upon this being found out, insisted upon their crossing to England, refusing to make a settlement upon her unless she was received in society here. She & her husband accordingly came, & the Duke of Devonshire gave this grand ball, to which most of the town went; but as no one spoke to her, I do not see that it will assist much in patching up her broken reputation.'[192]

Reputation was everything at this time and society was a harsh critic. Georgy's and William's mothers had every reason to be cautious of the match and the opinions it would invite. Even mutual friends of Georgy and William discussed their surprise at the announcement through gossipy letters. One excellent surviving example is from the former Pamela Fitzgerald, daughter of Lord Edward Fitzgerald. Pamela was a close confidante of William's, but although Georgy had played with her as a child but they had not remained close. The letter is addressed to Miss Eden, who in turn was also a friend and correspondent of Georgy's for many years:

> 'I was quite sorry I had sent my letter the day after I found out I was at liberty to talk about William de Roos's marriage. I am all delighted, and all that, and all I should be when I see him so happy. But tho' I have been going thro' all the palliating influence of confidant and in his secret, and within the mark of all hopes, and fears, and difficulties, yet I cannot shake off the idea that she is not good enough, he is selon moi such a dear creature, so much beyond the common run of man, of young men. Of course I rely on your keeping this alongside with your own ideas on the subject. I believe she is improved, and I liked her once, when first she came out, and you know we certainly sober in this world unless we go mad; perhaps she may have taken that turn. In short there is much

> in her favour, but while he was marrying a beggar he might have had a pleasanter, but opportunity does all those things, there is no choice in the case.'[193]

Lady Campbell certainly had the measure of Georgy as 'a beggar', as she had barely a penny to her name. Her opinion that Georgy was 'not good enough' for William, is further proof that her reputation had been tarred by her personal relationships with men. She had certainly enjoyed befriending members of the male sex, leaving her in a vulnerable position when it came to the opinion of her female contemporaries. Although she had female friends such as Miss Eden who she thought was 'charming and agreeable', Georgy had been more comfortable in her youth surrounded by military men and her female friendships had largely been left unattended. Equally William had many female friends who were passionately protective of him.

However, it was certainly true that the Lennoxes supported this union more than the one planned by Georgy's brother Lord William Pitt Lennox. His plan to marry the celebrated singer Mary Anne Paton was met with derision and anger from the Richmond clan. William was the son of a Duke and Mary was a lowborn stage performer, two sides of society that should never meet through marriage. Harking back to William Pitt Lennox's life in Ireland as a child, Wellington's comment that William should be sent to 'Covent Garden or Sadler's Wells' was surprisingly prophetic. Headstrong William could not be persuaded to simply take Mary as his mistress, believing himself to be totally in love with her. After they married his new wife continued to act under her maiden name. This was unheard of, and caused even greater disapproval from the Dowager Duchess. William did not mind in the slightest however as Mary's income was bringing in very necessary funds which far outweighed his own.

William and Georgy were married on 7th June 1824 in the fashionable St George's Church in Hanover Square, London, with all family members in attendance. As was tradition, many beautiful wedding presents were bestowed upon the couple. Wellington outdid them all by presenting the happy couple with a magnificent silver service set, inscribed 'The gift of the Duke of Wellington to Lady Georgiana de Ros on her marriage 7th June 1824'. Lady Bathurst wrote to Georgy 'The Duke talked of your silver dishes, they are bespoke & he thinks in gift for readiness,'[194] encouraging her to use them often in her new home.

However, the couple's first marital home left their beautiful wedding presents looking a little out of place. William was still only a Lieutenant so Georgy had to quickly reconcile herself to a restricted lifestyle until he was promoted. William was on Sir Colquhoun Grant's staff in Dublin and the two headed straight to the Royal Barracks there as soon as the wedding celebrations were complete, so that William could attend to his many military duties. Lady Campbell wrote: 'Is it not so like William de Roos to go to Ireland to avoid the wishing joy? He had business certainly, but still nobody but him could do such a thing.'[195] It must have been quite a shock for Georgy to be thrown into the role of military wife and find herself occupying a set of rooms rather than stately houses. Sir Colquhoun was a widower so she was called upon to do the honours at all his parties. She got into a 'terrible scrape' when she once sent the wife of a second major into dinner before the wife of the first.[196] Georgy rose to the challenge of being an army wife with her characteristic charm and confidence and was delighted to be back in Ireland, a country to which she had always attached fond memories.

As soon as the couple could they visited Strangford, where William had been entrusted as the estate's agent for some years. Georgy instantly fell in love with the stunning landscape of the Irish peninsula around the village. As remote as it was romantic, Strangford held in its grasp the promise of happiness and the prospect of building a new life with William. Finally escaping the clutches of her mother and the restrictions imposed on her as an unmarried woman, Georgy was blissfully happy. That summer was spent in the quiet idyll of country life away from London's wild parties. Whilst William busied himself building a rapport with the various tenants who lived on the de Ros estate, his wife took up gardening, a pursuit which quickly endeared her to her new in-laws. Her myrtles and fuchsias were a particular success and in years to come they became 'unusually large', and an object of great admiration to her children. Another contemporary observer reported that 'W. de Ros's marriage has turned out happily. He has become gardener, carpenter, mechanic, boatman, fisherman; in short always occupied and consequently always happy…it is a beau ideal of real happiness.'[197] Even Lady Campbell was won over. She reported to Miss Eden: 'William de Roos is the happiest of men, and Lady G. Lennox has won Uncle Henry's [Fitzgerald] heart by taking to gardening; I hope it may turn out well and [will] shame the Devil.'[198]

Georgy soon became pregnant and a girl named Frances Charlotte was born on 26th February 1825. William recorded in his diary that all were 'very happy & comfortable.'[199] By this time, the family had left Ireland and were living in small lodgings in Maidenhead. William was a fastidious writer, detailing all aspects of their life, including their domestic arrangements, which continued to be modest due to ongoing frictions with his family:

> 'My family now consists of G & Fanny now 10 months old, Jane her nurse (from Ireland) Sarah a maid who attends G & Mrs Thompson a soldiers wife who cooks & does housework- Leck & his boy in the stable, a good black horse for Cab. Judy & Jerry who carries G. Mrs Leck washes for us. My income is about 900 per annum... unpleasant discussion with my family just ended respecting an allowance. It is now settled that Ld Henry is to excuse me 100 per annum of the interest on my fortune (which he gave us to enable me to purchase my troop). This is equivalent to allowing me 100 a year. Little enough but they think otherwise & to avoid disputes I remain contented.'[200]

William, Georgy and Fanny would have to make do with this allowance as Lady de Ros continued to disapprove slightly of William's marriage. Lady Campbell wrote to Miss Eden: 'His family cannot forgive him for having picked out a little happiness for himself in his own way.'[201] Over time and as their family grew however, this disfavour with Lady de Ros would thaw.

Georgy and William's relationship blossomed and was full of love and affection. They were not able to celebrate their first wedding anniversary together but exchanged letters which show their closeness. 'I cannot tell you my very Dear William how nice & dear I thought & do think you were for writing me such a letter on that very day.'[202] Even the financial strains they were under did not take any toll on their relationship and Georgy appears to have embraced her new life with great energy. It is remarkable how well Georgy adapted to the reduced circumstances of her early married life from the grand drawing rooms of her youth. Showing a fortitude many had doubted of her, heightened by her first true period of happy independence as a married woman, she had never been more settled despite the large number of relocations she and William were required to endure.

When William's regiment next moved back to England they took a flat above a hairdresser's shop. There was a girl called Charlotte who worked in the establishment downstairs who the couple hired as Georgy's maid. Charlotte and Georgy became very close and she remained an integral part of the family unit for the next sixty years, living on with Georgy when she retired from work. In London their residence was in Regent's Park Barracks where they were allocated four rooms and a kitchen. The fact that Georgy was living in barracks caused 'conflicting opinions in London society.'[203] Whereas some highflyers such as Lady Bath expressed her 'admiration and approval' of such a practical and convenient arrangement, other women were forbidden by their husbands to visit Georgy at home.[204] Georgy found all this highly amusing and gamely re-engaged with London society, holding dinners in her cosy quarters on a regular basis. She continued her correspondence with her closest friends, including the Duke of Wellington, Lady Bathurst and Miss Eden; but her day to day life now revolved around her fledgling family.

Georgy and William's relationship was a stark contrast to the marriage of the Duke and Duchess of Wellington. Since their early years together there had been little intimacy between them. They now lived mostly separate lives, with Kitty spending most of the year at Stratfield Saye and rarely attending London's social scene. When Wellington was there he slept at the opposite end of the house. The Duchess was hopelessly unable to fulfil her role as the society hostess befitting the wife of the hero of Waterloo. Other female figures in Wellington's life were quick to fill Kitty's shoes including Lady Charlotte Greville and Marianne Patterson. After the death of her first husband, Marianne shocked everyone by marrying Wellington's brother Lord Wellesley. She continued to be a close friend of the Duke's, but not being able to marry her was probably one of the great regrets of his life.

In her place Wellington met and befriended Mrs Harriet Arbuthnot, a feisty brunette known for her political wit and quick humour. The two were seen together regularly but their relationship was purely platonic despite the rumours; some of which had been started by Charles Greville in an attempt to blacken Wellington's reputation. The Duke and Harriet paid no heed to these baseless rumours but agreed to reduce the amount of time they were seen out together. Wellington was also very close to Harriet's husband Charles Arbuthnot and after Harriet's sudden death in 1834 Charles came to live with him at Apsley House. Georgy and William were also close to the Arbuthnots. They dined in London, and the Arbuthnots stayed with them at Thames Ditton in 1834, just before Harriet was taken ill.

All his life Wellington liked to surround himself with strong women with independent minds. Kitty could not compete with the most confident, brilliant and well connected women of the age who all enjoyed being close to Wellington. Before her marriage, no doubt Georgy felt compelled to compete but now that her focus had shifted to her young family, she watched with interest as the role of Wellington's 'mistress' changed over these years. She was content to be a friend on the periphery and was happy that any suggestion of a romantic connection with the Duke had long been expunged. Indeed, Wellington's relationship with his female friends had changed. Gone were the frivolous and passionate affairs of the days of Waterloo. Now

Wellington required the companionship of an engaged and intelligent female mind and nothing more. Having known Wellington since the Peninsular days, Georgy felt secure in his affection for her, and no longer pursued the position of Wellington's right hand lady.

At the beginning of 1827 Georgy was again with child and William reported: 'This year finds me very happy in all my domestic concerns, setting out for Brighton where Georgiana will be confined about Febr when my regimental leave will be nearly expired, but I shall hope it gets prolonged.' Happily relations with his family were on the mend too. William continued that he had 'have never been on so comfortable terms with my own family as this month we staid [sic] with them at Boyle Farm, where the time passed in perfect harmony. When I look back on the sorrows of the last year I am thankful for the cheerfulness of my mind which I have recovered much more than I could have expected.'[205] The previous year his elder brother Arthur, a Lieutenant-Colonel in the Army, had died. This event was 'a most severe and irreparable loss,'[206] for the de Ros family and probably had a hand in bringing them closer together.

On 11th March Georgy, 'after suffering all day was delivered of a Boy at 10pm,'[207] whom they named Dudley. The family remained in Brighton for another month. William proudly recorded 'G is going on well & the child is thriving,'[208] but the happy family were now in need of a more permanent living arrangement. Relations with his family now restored, William went to his father to discuss the possibility of moving into a house on the Thames Ditton estate near Boyle Farm. In April Georgy and William went with Henry Fitzgerald to look over a small but charming cottage. William wrote that when Georgy saw the cottage she was 'much pleased & indeed it will be a most convenient little residence.'[209] The small cottage adjoined the Boyle Farm estate so the family could regularly visit each other and Georgy was thrilled with the arrangement.

The family still had regular contact with London society and with Wellington's circle of friends in particular. They often drove to London to dine with him or to attend the opera in his company. Wellington always kept his box free and would offer it to his closest friends at their convenience. The London season still caused much amusement and distraction for Georgy. However, the stresses of London life were summed up nicely by her friend Miss Eden who complained that the 'streets are not wide enough for the carriages, nor the week long enough for its engagements, there is not enough money to spend, nor sufficient time to spend it, not people enough to go to the dinners that are given, yet more than enough to fill the largest house that can be opened for them. In short such a mess! Puck was a clever fellow when he looked on and said, 'Oh, what fools these mortals be!'[210] More congenial visits included the de Ros family's annual trip to Stratfield Saye at Easter, together with various assorted members of Wellington's inner circle. From 1829 when Wellington became Lord Warden of the Cinque Ports, the autumn season was often spent at Walmer Castle where the Duke held a small and select court. It was by far his favourite residence and one that he visited increasingly as the years progressed.

The wild and unruly parties of Georgy's youth had now been replaced by more sophisticated evening events where Georgy could socialise with politicians and leading lights of the day. She and William were regular guests at dinners thrown by Lord Auckland, brother to Georgy's best friend Miss Eden, after he was appointed First Lord of the

Admiralty. Georgy always retained such 'interesting recollections of the pleasant dinner-parties at Lord Auckland's, where Brougham, Luttrell, Rogers, Lady Morley, Mr. George Villiers (afterwards Earl of Clarendon) and his accomplished sister, after Lady Theresa Lewis, were among the frequent guests.'[211] It was here that Georgy met Lord Melbourne, husband of the notorious Lady Caroline Lamb and future Prime Minister. Despite their differing political views, Melbourne became the Premier with whom Georgy was on the best terms. Her confidence and quick wit made her a very popular dinner guest and whether she sat at dinner with the Prime Minister or the latest great society beauty, she was always sure to keep them entertained.

Priscilla, Lady Burghersh, daughter of William Wellesley-Pole and niece of the Duke of Wellington, became another close friend of Georgy's. Intelligent and lively, Priscilla was Wellington's favourite niece and she in turn, adored her uncle. Despite the potential for Georgy and Priscilla to be jealous of each other's relationship with Wellington they actually became very close, a further illustration of the maturity of Georgy's relationship with the Duke. Both women had children of the same age who played together at Stratfield Saye and Walmer Castle. Priscilla was often abroad accompanying her husband who was a diplomat and therefore her youngest son Julian stayed with the de Ros family during his school holidays from Harrow. After one stay Priscilla wrote: 'A thousand thanks for your kind letter & account of dear Julian I hope the poor little fellow is getting more reconciled to school & I feel a real comfort in knowing that you are near him & kind to him- I cannot sufficiently thank you for all the kindness & feeling you have invariably shewn me.'[212] On another occasion Priscilla took on the role of intermediary for Wellington who had upset

Georgy over some small matter. She wrote: 'The Duke has desired me to ask you, if you are not too angry with him for his bad behaviour, if you would like to come to town on Monday next to dine with him at 6 o'clock and go afterwards to Madam Albertazzi's Benefit at Drury Lane, where all the Italian singers will sing. He will have a box.'[213] Although the Duke was well-known for his fierce and unpredictable temper, he was quick to forget and tended to offer an olive branch to the offended party in place of a face to face apology.

The strength of Georgy's character during these years lay in her ability to make friends with everyone from her own hairdresser to the Prime Minister. Nothing was too much trouble and she delighted in helping out her friends in any way she could, despite her own busy schedule and growing family. Her love for children meant it was easy for her to make more female friends than she had had before, as they now had their young families in common. Georgy and William still loved socialising, and were in London for most of the summer seasons whilst their children were young. Without the space to hold large parties of their own, they often stayed for periods of time at Boyle Farm, where splendid evening events were the norm.

One such party was held in the summer of 1827 which saw Boyle Farm and the de Ros family make it once again into London's society pages. Henry de Ros had set upon a plan to hold the most lavish and extravagant party to end all parties. He combined forces with his fellow hell-raisers Lord Alvanley, Lord Chesterfield, Lord Castlereagh and Lord Robert Grosvenor. Each contributed to the project the princely sum of £500 and Henry was in charge of all the preparations. He was the perfect man for the task as he never did anything in half measures and this extravaganza would be no exception. Henry managed to persuade his parents to host the party at Boyle Farm, considering it to be the perfect venue. Some five hundred people were invited and competition for a ticket was fierce. When in London, people constantly asked Henry to dinner, in the hope that he would be forced to issue them with an invite. This happened so regularly that Henry would often have to pretend not to see people he knew for fear of being obliged to ask them.[214] Miss Eden confirmed Henry's rise to social favourite: 'I remember about four years ago when the Sarpent [Henry] came gliding into Almack's- and no woman spoke to him, and he-even the Sarpent's own self, looked daunted; and now he sent out his cards naming on them the pretty sister of the family.'[215] Henry had managed to regain his reputation after the scandal of his illegitimate child. His precious invitations even included costume patterns with instructions, dictating what each person was to wear and what role they would have in the evening's proceedings. One particularly amusing incident recalled by Miss Eden involved the Baring family: 'at nine o'clock the night before the breakfast, [Henry] apologised for not having been able to spare an invitation for them before, and added "the only condition is a new gown; I believe there is still time for that." They went! In new gowns! I believe there was never a more beautiful breakfast when all was done- those sort of men will succeed!'[216]

On the evening of the event everyone arrived wearing their finest and most expensive clothes, some having only been finished a few hours previously. A sumptuous meal was enjoyed by four hundred and fifty guests under a tent on the lawn whilst they were serenaded by musicians. As the lights dimmed the finest singers of the day were ferried up and down the Thames on gondolas, their voices carrying on the wind to the party. The groves dotted around the lawn and lakes were illuminated with different coloured lamps twinkling in the evening light. Spectacular fireworks filled the sky as night fell. Georgy and William's sister Olivia were included in the opening quadrille, as twenty-six of the prettiest girls, including the 'Foresters, Brudnells, De Rooses, Mary Fox, [and] Miss Russell,'[217] opened the evening's dancing. Each were dressed as 'Rosieres', traditionally young village girls chosen for their beauty and virtue. Although Georgy had recently given birth to Dudley she had been convinced to perform by Henry. *The Times* reported that 'the principal charm was the brilliant appearance of a temporary room, where 24 of the loveliest ladies in London enchanted every eye by the elegant fancy of their dress, and the harmonious grace of their motion in a quadrille costumee.'[218] It must have been a sparkling and memorable evening. Miss Eden concluded 'It never came out in a finer manner...Everyone seemed pleased with it. What stories may have risen from it have not yet transpired. And Mr. de Roos [William] said to Lady Jersey, he trusted the whole thing had been done most correctly- he should be miserable if there could be even a surmise of the slightest impropriety....!'[219] Luckily no such impropriety made it from the lawns of Boyle Farm to the pages of *The Times* when they reported on the party the following week.

Wellington did not attend the famous Boyle Farm party. Since returning to England permanently after the Army of Occupation had been disbanded in 1818, the Duke had been drawn further into the political epicentre of Whitehall and was always extremely busy. Highly knowledgeable in all military matters and loved by the people, political leaders hoped that he could sprinkle some of his popularity on the unstable social issues of the time. Discontent was sweeping both the town and countryside. The masses called for reform, to which most of the government were emphatically opposed. In 1828 Wellington was invited by George IV to become Prime Minister. Wellington agreed and reluctantly relinquished his position as Commander in Chief of the Army as it was felt that not even he could fulfil both roles. Although he had no personal ambition to be Prime Minister, he saw that the current situation could easily become unmanageable without confident leadership. Yet there was also the Duke's health to consider, which was far from stable. Working himself into the ground on a regular basis, he also suffered with his hearing after a botched ear operation a few years previously. Lady Bathurst wrote to Georgy that year: 'I hear Sir Henry Halford says the Duke of Wellingtons recovery must be a work of time, but he looks to the possibility of its being entire, I hope he may be right, but he can never be the same again, for he can scarcely recover his looks after 50, when they have been so altered & cannot recover his deafness, however if he could regain his sleep that wd be an essential thing.'[220]

In June 1830 King George IV died and his brother the Duke of Clarence became King William IV. Georgy and William had known the Duke and Duchess of Clarence when they had resided close to them in Bushy Park. Now, with a coronation pending and the elevation of the Duke's position, Georgy and William found themselves invited to dine in splendour in London. The Duke of Clarence was a much loved figure, despite having always lived in the shadow of his older and more extravagant brother George IV. The new King had always taken a great interest in the minutiae of other peoples' lives. He once met Georgy unexpectedly when she was on her way to Kingston. Enquiring where she was going, Georgy replied 'To Kingston, sir' 'And what are you going to buy?' 'Petticoats for the children, sir' and she then had the greatest difficulty in preventing him accompanying her on her errand. William's sister Olivia de Ros was appointed Maid of Honour to Queen Adelaide. She went on to marry Henry Wellesley, Wellington's brother, who later became Lord Cowley. When the ceremony took place at Windsor Castle in 1833, the King gave the bride away and a huge banquet was thrown for the newly married couple, which William and Georgy attended. Thus the Fitzgerald- de Ros and Wellesley families were now formally joined in marriage, creating an even closer bond between them than ever before.

It was during his tenure as Prime Minster that Wellington undertook massive alterations to Apsley House, the Robert Adam mansion that he had purchased from his brother Richard in 1817. Lodging in No.10 Downing Street during this period, he added two bays to either side of the house. A new gallery was designed to house his impressive collection of Old Master paintings, much of which had been captured from Joseph Bonaparte's carriage after the Battle of Vitoria in 1813. It was taken to London after the battle and remained with Wellington as a generous gift from the King of Spain. Each year on the anniversary of the Battle of Waterloo the Duke held a banquet for the officers who had fought with him in honour of what they had achieved and the men they had lost. After the extensions on the house were completed the number of attendees was increased and the splendour of the evening was enhanced by shimmering chandeliers casting their light over the red walls of the Banqueting Hall. The table was laid with the stunning Portuguese table setting gifted to the Duke in thanks by the Portuguese nation, which Georgy recorded showing her two eldest children in 1836: 'I took Fan and Dudley up to town to see the Duke's Plate laid out for Waterloo Dinner. He shewed [sic] it us himself.'[221]

In his politics Wellington was conservative but not inflexible. Although he was renowned for his opposition to electoral reform, his main achievement from his time in office was to push through the Catholic Emancipation Bill which had been hotly contested for years by the conservative majority in the House of Lords. It was clear to Wellington that peace could not be sustained in Ireland if Roman Catholics were not given the same political representation as those of other religions, which is what the bill bravely championed. However, the British people were more interested in the comprehensive emancipation of the middle classes than religious representative reform. To this the Iron Duke could not, and would not, agree. Forcing the Catholic Emancipation Bill into law caused such a collapse within the Tory party that in 1830 Wellington was forced to resign. The Great Reform Act, emancipating tens of thousands of new voters, came into law two years later, changing the face of political representation forever.

Wellington's opposition to class electoral reform caused widespread riots and for the first time in his life he found himself to be universally unpopular with those who had for so long idolised him. His politics were now seen as outmoded and out of touch. Apsley House was attacked and windows were broken, forcing Wellington to install iron railings to keep the mob out. Wellington found this particularly upsetting as the Duchess of Wellington was taken dangerously ill at this time. As the weeks progressed her illness worsened, but in that time, the couple managed at last to find peace with each other. Kitty passed away on 24th April 1831, surrounded by her husband's medals and awards. He remarked sadly, 'How strange it was that people could live together for half a lifetime and only understand each other at the end.'[222] She was faithful to him to the last and despite their differences, Wellington felt her loss acutely. His relationship with his two sons Douro and Charles was often difficult and at best distant as he had been absent for much of their childhood. Both had adored their mother and had witnessed their father's unsympathetic and at times, cruel, treatment of her. They also felt an enormous pressure growing up as the children of the great Duke of Wellington.

Wellington certainly found it easier to communicate with his friend's children, in fact he enjoyed their company enormously. With them he was able to relax in a way he never could with his own and his kindness to children was well known. Georgy wrote of one such occasion 'when he invited his friends to visit him, their children were always included; and on one occasion, passing through the room where some of the juvenile guests were at tea (I rather think the present Premier was one!) he was very angry at finding they had no jam, and instantly gave orders it was never to be omitted!'[223] When Georgy would come down for dinner with the other adults they usually discovered the Duke had dressed early and come down to engage 'in a regular game of romps with the children, who came down on purpose for what they called the Battle of Waterloo, which commenced by one of them throwing a cushion at the newspaper the Duke was reading.'[223a] Wellington would then fly at them in false fury, and the children would scatter around the house shrieking with laughter. Charles Arbuthnot wrote to Georgy 'Your letter amused the Duke very much. I delight in Blanche's collecting a circle about her and telling everybody that she had found out the secret of the Duke's doing his battles so well from his making such good shots with the cushions.'[224]

Georgy brought Frances and Dudley to see the Duke whenever she could and when she gave birth to another baby the Duke was named godfather. The girl's name was Blanche, and her first middle name was Georgina, after Georgy's beloved aunt the Lady Bathurst. Her second middle name was Arthur, after Wellington. This has been interpreted by some as a thinly veiled reference to Blanche's true parentage. In truth it was simply a way for Georgy to celebrate her friendship with the Duke as well as the fact that he had agreed to be Blanche's godfather. He wrote to Georgy 'My dearest Georgy, I sincerely congratulate you. I am much flattered by your desire to call the young lady Arthur, and shall be delighted to be her godfather.'[225] It was a rather unusual way for Georgy to pay tribute to the Duke.

Cherished by their parents, the de Ros children grew strong and boisterous from the many months they spent playing on the shores of the Strangford lough. Georgy reflected in her diary that 'The Duke often told me that my children were better behaved then I was as a child,'[225a] which is not difficult to imagine when thinking back to the years of the unruly Lennox clan causing havoc in every house they occupied. Wellington was particularly fond of Blanche, who grew to idolise him, and no doubt reminded him of her mother. He must have had a sense of history repeating itself when he met with Georgy and her bright-eyed and animated children. When Blanche was five she worked a pin cushion for the Duke which Georgy sent to him. A little time passed with no reply and so Georgy sent him a note of friendly complaint. He then replied: 'I recollect that Blanch has as much, if not more, reason to complain of my neglect than you have. I enclose a note to her.' The charming note read 'Dearest Blanch, I am very much obliged for your beautiful present. I shall be able to keep my pins, which your mamma will tell you were heretofore stolen! But I admire your writing still more than your work.'[226]

However, the happy family was soon to be separated when William was summoned to work abroad. It would be a trying time for all of them, especially for Georgy who was reminded of her father's death on foreign shores. But as has been demonstrated on countless occasions, Georgy's strength of character, her ability to adapt to every situation and ultimately her love for her husband would carry her through the difficult months of separation.

CHAPTER NINE

Adventures out East

'I wonder at myself for praising the wind which is taking me farther from you at such a rate, but it will be all the sooner over...I quite long to see your dear handwriting again...'[227]

Lord William de Ros to Lady Georgiana de Ros

In the wider political world rumblings from the East had long unsettled those in Westminster. Wellington's victory at Waterloo had heralded a period of peace and prosperity but Russia's threat was still acute. For centuries the Tsars had gazed longingly at the expanses of the East, from Persia to India, as sources of untapped wealth and commercial opportunity. The 1830s were no different. The British government felt rightly threatened by this vast power and so had from the early years of the nineteenth century sent officers into the unknown and unchartered territories of the East India Company's furthest outposts on reconnaissance trips. Their missions were to uncover new lands where a British presence could be exploited. Many returned with detailed maps and local information which had been surreptitiously recorded during their travels. The men knew they would have little or no protection once under cover and many went out East with the understanding that they could easily succumb to disease or violence; indeed, many did. Those that did return often recounted their adventures in print, sparking a new wave of interest. Ordinary people were fascinated by tales of the wild lands of the East, from Turkey to Afghanistan. The middle classes happily consumed even the most amateurish recollections of places and people they could barely visualise. The lands described were so strange and sublime that these publications must have carried in their pages a fantastical and even fictional flair. It would soon be time for William's words to be added to their number.

William had been informed that he was to travel to the Black Sea, a land-locked expanse of water in south-eastern Europe, bordering modern day Romania as well the Ukraine, Russia and Turkey. It was an area of special interest to the British as the Russians had already claimed several regions for their own and there was a need to know more about their military capabilities there. It was decided that a British contingent would be sent to this area under the guise of a gentlemanly diplomatic trip. Lord Palmerston, Secretary for Foreign Affairs, took the decision to send one Army and one Naval officer to make a tour of the area. William was chosen as he had proven himself to be a reliable and hardworking officer who was well liked and respected by his peers. The Navy representative was Lord Drinkwater and the two became close friends during the trip. Through a facade of official visits, military reviews and diplomatic soirées, the trip's true purpose was to ascertain the exact capabilities of the Russian military through these eastern outposts. William was to accompany Lord Durham in this official capacity, who was not to know of William's true mission.

William was given only two days' notice to prepare for the expedition. As he rushed to pack his bags and say goodbye to his family, in a touching gesture of filial love, his brother Henry gave him a coat and jacket for the long cold nights. Georgy gave him a miniature portrait of herself and one of their daughter Fanny, now eight years old. In their ten years of marriage never had William had to leave Georgy for so long and she was left greatly shaken by his departure. The lands through which he would be travelling were as unknown to William as the wilds of Canada had been to the 4th Duke of Richmond before his tragic demise, so the separation stirred up painful memories for Georgy. Fortunately, William had always been a committed letter-writer and had plenty of time on board to write home. He recorded much of his trip 'independent to official reports which I sent home from time to time' in the form of diary entries to Georgy: 'My dearest G, I suppose I had better write a little account every day, that when opportunities do occur I may send you a more full account of my proceedings.'[228] These long accounts in William's beautifully clear handwriting lay in a drawer for eighteen years before he decided to publish them. In the publication he described his account as 'a faithful and plain narrative of the expedition', and plain it certainly is. Anyone hoping for juicy titbits of illicit information from this undercover spy is left most unsatisfied. The original letters to Georgy are far warmer and fortunately they are all preserved in the family archive. Reading through the letters at William's father's desk on the family estate in Ireland almost two hundred years later there is a very real sense of William's devotion to his 'Dearest G'.

Due to the nature of his trip William's letters home were often limited to local sights and stories of only moderate interest to a modern reader. William had warned his brother Henry to expect 'but a dull letter'[229] from him, but in fact his long accounts of his expedition have a real charm to them and bring to life what an adventure travel was at the time. William found his letter writing a comforting connection to the life he had left behind and he regularly assured Georgy how hard their parting had been for him. He constantly enquired after Georgy, her health and the health of the children. He asked for details of the minutiae of their lives to fill the many dull days at sea in male company. Georgy replied regularly, but unfortunately William did not keep her letters as he had to travel light. It is clear in his replies to Georgy however that her letters stirred in William warm and sometimes even painful memories of home.

Resigned to an enforced separation from her husband, Georgy tried to make the best of the situation. She busied herself with the children and spent much of her time in London where distractions were plentiful. William had left her under the care of the ever devoted Lady Bathurst and her daughter Georgina, who had always been like a sibling to Georgy. Georgina's father Lord Bathurst had died that year and her brother Seymour during the previous one, so the two women were grateful to each other for company and distraction. William had written in his diary at the time of Seymour's death: 'most unexpectantly heard of poor Seymour B's sudden death this morning or last night in London- came home immediately. Poor G she loved him like a brother & I as a very dear friend- but poor Lord & Lady Bathurst.'[230]

William knew to send all his letters to the Bathurst's London address and he now wrote to Georgy a long letter from his private cabin. Comparing his quarters there to his private study at their cottage in Thames Ditton, he wrote that 'I have been writing & reading and examining…for the last 3 hours in my cabin as much alone & as quiet as in my little room at Ditton.' He continued that, having implored Georgy not to dwell on their separation, he must now do the same 'I must not talk of that till I am on way home to my dearest wife & children or I shall be acting contrary to all my injunctions to you.'[231]

Mostly William longed for a letter from Georgy '…I suppose there is a chance of my finding a letter from you telling me what are your plans, & how far you have attended to my charge of either going somewhere or having [a] friend to stay with you.'[232] He later wrote 'Need I tell you how much I thought of home yesterday & the value of the good little wife I had left there, while I walked up & down the deck after sunset with the odious fast wind still keeping us back, but to day a fine westerly wind has sprung up & put every body more or less in better heart.'[233] The separation was just as hard, if not harder, for William as it was for Georgy as he did not have the distractions of friends and a social life to fill his days. He would gaze upon the miniatures of Georgy and Frances longingly and crave news of their everyday domestic life. 'I have frequently pulled out my miniature of you and Fan & wish I had others of my dear Dudley & Blanch. I hope they are not too much for you, what I would give to have them in their noisiest & most restless mood for a few hours in my Cabin.'[234] In contrast to

Wellington's relationship with his wife, whose relationship had been reduced to correspondence about household matters a long time ago, William longed to know about the mundane details of Georgy's life back home with the children. He was a family man committed to the wellbeing of his wife and children. Georgy reassured him in her returning letter that she and the children were quite well, and that the true purpose of William's mission remained a secret known only to a few. None of their friends or acquaintances had heard any rumours of William's mission from Lord Palmerston. Soon Georgy was spending a lot of time with Henry and Olivia de Ros, who were also staying in London. Receiving reams of William's calm and measured handwriting at intervals throughout these difficult months was a huge comfort to Georgy.

On board the ship there was a convivial atmosphere: 'We breakfast at 8 & dine at 3 &, if there are none of the exercises of the ship privy on, everyone walks on deck, or sits in his Cabin & reads with as little interruption as is one's own home.'[235] Towards the end of August William reached Athens, which did not please him. He wrote:

> 'My dearest G, Yesterday Ogilvie & I went ashore together, at the Pixus, & getting on a couple of miserable ponies, rode up to Athens & proceeded to the Acropolis. It is certainly a very curious & singular place, & the Parthenon which stands in the middle of the fortress a noble piece of antiquity. But it loses much effect I think from the confusion of the scene, for up to the very foot of the hill are those half formed battered hovels…There are no remains of the roof of the Parthenon, & in the middle of its floor there is a paltry little Turkish mosque.'[236]

On his onward journey towards the Black Sea, William was shocked at what he saw of the living conditions of the poor: 'Huts built of loose boards, mud hovels, tents such as a gipsy would despise, all huddled together in disorder filth, and confusion' and describing the people as 'dirty, half-starved' and 'squatting about as in Ireland'. On the whole he was not impressed with the military camps he was shown, although Constantinople had a more lasting effect: 'The appearance of Constantinople is so very unlike anything else, that all descriptions I have read of this extraordinary place convey a very imperfect notion of the reality...' In Constantinople William met the Sultan and was relieved to report that he had 'given up the system of strangling and beheading, and does his utmost to govern this extraordinary nation on milder principles'. The Sultan was 'rather fat, and short; not handsome, but he has a pleasant and almost good-humoured smile.'[237] The party regularly dined in the Sultan's magnificent palace which was exquisitely furnished in a fashion that William had never seen before. He wrote that: 'The floors are inlaid wood of the finest kind, the walls painted & decorated with patterns, wreathes of flowers, & light beautiful canopy & fretted work...The Furniture and Draperies very handsome but all of a light texture with silks & muslins of the gayest description.'[238] William was however still pining for Georgy, staying for hours in his room, 'It is one of the faults of your little picture that there is a certain look of melancholy which I cannot clear from my countenance, as I usually can from that of the dear original & as I hope to do again, whichever vexation disturbs that quiet face of which I am so fond. But this will not do, I shall fancy myself as home instead of being in this distant country...'[239]

After Constantinople, in mid-September, the party reached Odessa where they enjoyed palatial dining every evening. They joined parties of over a hundred people and William laughingly reported that the 'Russian mode of serving dinner is after all but a pretext for eating double, and the majority of the guests stuffed themselves on this occasion till I almost expected their tight uniforms to give way under the pressure.'[240] In Kiev they met the Emperor where William makes his first brief mention of military fortification of the city: 'The arsenal is a noble building, erected by the Empress Catherine...It contains fifty thousand muskets and twenty thousand sabres and lances; also field –battery and horse-artillery guns, to the amount of three hundred and twenty pieces.'[241] He later reported: 'The probable object of fortifying this inland city is to establish a good place of assembly for troops and reserves...Kiev is the seat of government of the province of 'Little Russia,' and is always with a large garrison.' From the end of September to late December, there were no letters from William meaning Georgy did not know where her husband was. The worry and the anguish had a serious and detrimental effect on her health. Despite her entreaties to William's colleagues in the Army, nothing could be found of his whereabouts. Until a letter made its way through, she had absolutely no idea as to whether something terrible had happened to her beloved husband.

Unbeknown to Georgy, William had travelled safely from Kiev to Bucharest, and was now intent on getting home as soon as possible. It was felt that the useful objectives had been fulfilled from the trip and William was keen to get back to England before many of the routes home became impassable during winter. Finally, a letter made it to London and contained much hope that he would be home soon, 'The road home looks long upon the map, but now that we have once fairly begun it, all the fatigue & annoyance will daily diminish.'[242] He impressed upon Georgy to tell the children the reason for the absence in letters was only that he had been too busy to write: 'Tell my dear Fan & Dudley that it is only a want of time which has prevented my writing oftener to them, but when we stop in this way for a couple of days there is so much to do in visiting the authorities, & preparing for another start, that one seldom gets a quiet hour except early or late.'[243] He wrote to Henry the next day 'it is satisfactory to have thoroughly accomplished at last every object intended & to be on ones way home. I will not bore you will all the details of our direction, but content myself with saying that we have been upset 5 times, & wrecked a carriage, a sledge, & finally a regular waggon.'[244] The roads were proving as treacherous as William had feared. He estimated he would arrive around the middle of January, 'What a happy day it will be' he exclaimed.[245] By the 12th December he had reached Vienna 'being at last in a civilised country,'[246] where he saw Lord Douro; Wellington's eldest son and now a close friend of the family.

Whilst William had been adventuring with Sultans and Emperors, Georgy socialised with friends and family. She saw her friends including the Duke of Wellington when he was in London, but as the months passed her poor health meant that she was often confined to the house. When William finally returned to England in late January 1835, Georgy went to meet him off the boat. It must have been a huge relief to be reunited but William was shocked at the change in his wife, as their six months' separation had markedly changed her features. Lady Bathurst who had seen Georgy suffering and knew that William would be worried to see her so changed, wrote to him:

> 'It is a great Blessing to have you home safe & well my Dear William. I hope you are not disappointed with dear little G's

> looks, though I daresay her Constant Anxiety and above all the intense anxiety of the last few days have caused a care worn Expression, for I verily believe that she Experienced what we have been told that "Hope delayed makes the heart sick".

Lady Bathurst continued that she hoped William enjoyed getting reacquainted with the children who had grown tremendously and were delighted to be returned to their papa. Of bold and opinionated Blanche she wrote 'I wonder to how Baboo [Blanche] likes you for no doubt she has herself informed you of the Exact truth on that subject and many others'. Of Fanny she concludes that she had grown into a beautiful young woman in her father's absence, creating 'mischief' with the men that she had been meeting when out with her mother. 'It was lucky for you that you did not see Fanny at Wood End. She was so remarkably well there & grew so very pretty that you would have never thought it necessary to take steps to immediately counter act the mischief that a brilliant complexion & many other of her dear attributes accessioned.'[247] Like her mother, Fanny was fast becoming a ballroom favourite, similarly uninterested in making fast her attraction to one man.

So William returned to England to find that his children were growing up. Blanche was the most outspoken of the three, whilst her sister Fanny was becoming a great beauty. Dudley, who idolised his father and had missed him the most of all, was thrilled to have him back. He had spent many a day playing with a model ship William had given him before he had left, imagining the adventures his father was experiencing. William was delighted and relieved to be back with the people he loved most and soon settled back into family life. Although he was not one to show off about his adventures out East, he could not resist regaling his family with stories of the places he had visited and the extraordinary characters he had met. During those cold winter months back in England, sitting around the fireside, the de Ros children would gather to hear his stories. Their favourite story was when William would tell how he made notes of the Sebastopol fortifications on his shirt-sleeve so as not to blow his cover to the Russians. Sebastopol would later play host to a year long siege between the Allies and the Russians during the Crimean War, forming one of the most famous and crucial acts after the catastrophic Battle of Balaklava.

Meanwhile the family made plans to return to Ireland so that Georgy could recover her health. However, it was not to be the quiet idyll of country life that William and his family so desperately sought. A few months later a scandal broke which shook the reputation of his family and the good name of de Ros to their core.

CHAPTER TEN

Scandal

He puts on an appearance of softness & modesty such as one never saw, & is in reality the most profligate good for nothing in the Kingdom'[247a]

Mrs Harriet Arbuthnot on Henry de Ros

Rumours had been circulating for months that Henry de Ros's gambling habits had taken a sinister turn. Georgy had done her best to ignore the whispers that reached her but it is likely that this added pressure, which of course she could not share with William whilst he was away, contributed to her ill health. Henry's behaviour at the various gambling dens and gentlemen's clubs which he frequented had roused suspicion. Henry had been playing a sleight of hand card trick called sauter-le-coup, where a marked card is dealt from the bottom of the pack. This behaviour was not only illegal but totally unacceptable. Those who frequented London's most exclusive and prestigious clubs started to whisper of Henry's deceit. Although well practised at drinking and gambling to excess, subtlety and discretion were not two of Henry's strong points. Rumours of his double-dealings circulated amongst his friends, many of whom had also been victims of his treachery. However, Henry's popularity meant that several friends tried to warn him by sending anonymous letters imploring him to stop this deceit, but he was addicted and carried on. It was hoped by many that the scandal would pass and that he would have the sense to escape the country until things had blown over but Henry stubbornly denied the claims and refused to retreat.

After William returned from his adventures on the Black Sea and discovered what was happening, he forced Henry to admit the severity of the situation despite believing his claims of innocence. William convinced Henry to escape the rumours until they blew over and to head to Germany. Henry's great friend Charles Greville recorded in his diary:

> 'When I got back to London I found it all ringing with the de Ros's affair to which I have never been able to bring myself to allude...To have one's oldest and most intimate friend convicted of being a cheat and a swindler, to be compelled to believe that for a long course of years he has been practicing this nefarious trade, and that I have been not infrequently myself one of his victims, while his accusers are also my intimate friends and near relations is quite enough to cloud the most cheerful prospect. His is now threatening to return here and meet charges which must overwhelm him; God knows how it will end...'[248]

Greville was appalled at the convincing evidence set before him of his friend's embarrassing fall from grace. He had even been sent one

Henry's marked cards, evidence that could not be denied. Toying with the card, Greville pondered Henry's fate. It was unlikely that his friend would ever been formally charged but his reputation was as good as ruined. Before Greville could act an article appeared in *The Satirist* exposing the scandal to the public gaze. The de Ros family and their friends tried to close ranks and contain the situation but society was buzzing with the story and Henry was drawing more attention to himself by 'vehemently and solemnly' asserting his innocence.[249]

When news reached the Duke of Wellington he tried to use his considerable influence to clear Henry's name. Greville wrote that the Duke had taken a 'very violent part in his [Henry's] defence.'[250] Wellington, as something of a master of public relations, understood how best to manage the situation. He wrote regularly to Georgy, stating that his main concern was that Henry would try to take matters into his own hands:

> 'Dearest Georgy, I have received your note and I perfectly understand the State in which Lord de Ros' affair stresses. Indeed I expected it would be so. It is quite obvious that every thing that is done is known to the whole World and of course for both the Parties...I earnestly recommend that Lord de Ros...has determination upon his course and has retained Counsel to have no communication with any body whatsoever until his Case excepting his Counsel. Every communication which he will make to any body will be for the benefit of those who are his adversaries upon this Subject.'[251]

In his next letter he implored her to impress upon Henry that 'There is no case upon which the "Golden Rule" of Silence is not important for its success!'[252]

Henry's greatest supporters were his brother William and his brother-in-law Henry Wellesley, who now gathered around him. In private perhaps both had their doubts that Henry was innocent, but in public they maintained this belief to protect not only him but the family name. They were also desperately worried about Henry's health which had been a serious concern for a number of years. The stress of such public exposure was beginning to show. William, Henry Wellesley and the Duke of Wellington advised Henry de Ros to return to London to bring legal action against his accusers. William and the Duke were sure that there was not enough evidence to convict Henry but wanted to have his name cleared by prosecuting those who had written and circulated these rumours. Only then could Henry's reputation be regained. It was a bleak winter spent in Strangford as the scandal rumbled on. Finally, in February Henry took one of his accusers, a Mr Cumming, to court for libel:

> 'The trial excited much interest; and among the distinguished persons present were Lords Lyndhurst, Alvanley, and Wharncliffe. It was charged against Lord de Ros, that at the whist table he frequented contrived to have a violent fit of coughing when his deal came, which obliged him to put his hands under the table; and then it always happened that he turned up an honour, and that the aces and kings in the packs Lord de Ros played with, were frequently marked, slightly but perceptibly, with the thumb-nail. Many gentlemen swore to their having been cheated by these tricks, and some refused to play with Lord de Ros, though others did not shun him after his cheating had been discovered- they sent him anonymous notes of warning, and hoped that he had left off cheating. The play of these gentlemen was very high sometimes; and one of them, Mr Brook Greville, admitted, that he [Henry] had made £35,000 [£4,200,000] by play; another, Captain Alexander,

> said, that he was a 'better man by £10,000 [£1,200,000] for card-playing.'[252a]

The public nature of the scandal was difficult for Georgy to bear. She went to tea with her friend Lady Salisbury, who reported: 'She is quite overwhelmed. But I am glad to find that she seems prepared of the course her friends must necessarily take on this sad occasion, and does not expect or wish her brother-in-law to be received.'[253] In the circumstances, Henry could no longer be accepted in the households of any of his friends.

Greville was called as a witness for the defence, much to the horror of the Wellesley and de Ros families. Although a fellow gambler Greville was a well-known and respected society figure and his opinion would weigh heavily. William wrote to Greville to try and convince him not to give evidence at the trial, fearing that such a damning character witness could lead to Henry's case being thrown out. He threatened Greville with 'the loss of his friendship' and the 'indignation of society'[254] if he did attend. Yet even if Greville had decided not to give his testimony, the evidence against Henry was indisputable. His only defence was that he had stiffness in the joints of the fingers which prevented him from playing card tricks. The jury was not fooled by this rather lame defence and took only fifteen minutes to throw Henry's case out of court. Greville and Lord Alvanley, another of Henry's friends, went to de Ros straight after the trial. Greville 'found him in a very miserable plight and very obstinate....I entered the room brimful of pity, feeling ashamed for him and melted to entire softness, but before I had been there 5 minutes, in spite of his agony, which was apparent, I felt hard as iron, for I saw that his suffering did not proceed from a source calculated to excite compassion or tender regret.'[255]

Henry was furious that his good character had been ruined and never saw that he had manufactured his own destruction. He retreated to France, as was common for those who had created either scandal or huge debts. The affair took such an attack on his health that he would never truly recover.

After the affair was over Georgy and William visited Stratfield Saye. Lady Salisbury recorded in her diary the Duke's kindness in postponing any other visitors at this difficult time: 'Colonel and Lady Georgiana de Ros and their children came today. With his usual consideration, the Duke had not asked anyone to meet them for the first day or two. She looks ill, and he seems depressed, but shook it off a good deal after being here a short time.'[256] After recovering from the shock of the scandal on the Duke's estate, the de Ros family spent much of the summer in Ireland before returning to London. In September 1838 they visited the Duchess of Cambridge at Hampton Court where Blanche and Princess Mary played together.[257] Meanwhile a grand coronation was being organised for the new Queen Victoria who was just eighteen years of age. Georgy recorded in her diary: 'Took the children to Apsley House to see the [Coronation] Procession, I saw the Duke in his robes. Frank Egerton and Ernest Fane his Pages. Dined at the Bathursts and went to a grand ball at Apsley House. Soult and all the Foreigners there, very grand.'[258]

From London Georgy, Fanny and Blanche spent a month with the Duke of Wellington at Walmer Castle. This favourite residence of the Duke's had been his since his appointment to Lord Warden of the Cinque Ports in 1829. A large but modest castle situated on the stunning Kent coastline, it was the place where the Duke enjoyed escaping from his many official duties in London. Fortunately, Blanche saved

Georgy's diary entries from this period which provide wonderful insight into life at the castle and the continuing friendship between Wellington and Georgy. Different friends of Wellington's visited whilst Georgy and her family were there including Charles Arbuthnot, the Maryboroughs, the Fitzroy-Somersets, Sir Arthur Paget, and Princess Sophia of Gloucester. The de Ros family left in the middle of October 'having spent a most agreeable month there.'[259]

The following year Georgy was at one of her regular month long visits to Stratfield Saye, the Duke's estate in Hampshire. One evening she settled down at her writing desk and penned an account of the day to William, to whom she often wrote long gossipy letters similar to the ones she once sent to the Duke. Georgy wrote that Blanche had as usual 'posted herself on the Duke's knees- & talked quantities to him.'[260] Also staying at the house were Lord and Lady Tweeddale and their beautiful but shy daughter Elizabeth. Wellington's eldest son Douro was deeply in love with Elizabeth and had invited her family to meet his father which must have been a nerve-wracking experience. Georgy reported that:

> 'Ly Tweeddale quite delighted to find a friend here in me. Ly Elizabeth looked very shy poor girl, but very handsome, & the Duke's manner is so paternal & kind to her...Tuesday night- Our evening has gone off well considering that Ly Elizth is very shy, & Ly Tweeddale a little frightened at the Duke. Douro devoted himself to Lady Tweeddale & I think worried the poor girl...The Duke talked Peninsular talk with Ld Tweeddale, & a little Court talk with me'

The image of the Duke, a kindly gentleman, listening to a child's chatter whilst making every attempt to put a potential daughter-in-law at ease is an endearing one. Wellington had a strong desire to look after and to provide wise counsel to those he held most dear. This desire was far-reaching and extended way beyond the cosy comfort of the drawing room. Indeed, it extended to a great number of people, from all walks of life, and even to the new, young and attractive monarch, Queen Victoria. She had recently fallen under the control of the Prime Minister Lord Melbourne, for whom Wellington harboured a great distrust but who was friends with Georgy:

> 'He tormented himself over the state of affairs at Court, & said it was all owing to Ld Melbourne not having strength of mind or principle enough to tell the Q. that she must be on good terms with her mother [The Duchess of Kent, with whom she famously did not get on]. He talked with the greatest possible compassion of her, & with gloom of the state of Politics- saying that things were in such a mess that he did not see how it was ever to be got right.'[261]

The Queen, like Georgy, looked up to the Duke as a father figure. Perhaps Wellington in turn saw Lord Melbourne as a threat to that highly revered position.

William had planned to be with his wife at Stratfield Saye for this dinner but was instead with his brother in St. John's Wood. Henry had returned to his house there after the cheating affair had finally blown over, although since the trial he had been ostracised from London society. The reason for William's last minute change of plan was that Henry was desperately ill again and had returned to London to be closer to his family. Years of fast-living and hard drinking had taken their toll on him. The Queen recorded in her diary in January that Greville had reported on Henry's situation to Lord Melbourne:

> 'Lord M. said it was a peculiar kind of dropsy, wind and water; talked of his having no feeling about dying or religion; said, I thought it was better for his friends, he should die; "much better for his friends, and better for himself", said Lord M. "It was such a very bad case; he was a very agreeable man," continued Lord M., "I knew him very intimately". So, I said, did Uncle Leopold; and Lord M. said he had a much worse character abroad than here, for some time.'[262]

Both William and the Duke felt that the debacle of the previous year had been an unnecessary blot on the reputation of a man who had, without doubt, lived live to the full. Georgy wrote from Stratfield Saye: 'I trust that you are not low & that he is tolerably easy and comfortable. Tell him the Duke asked himself [acknowledged] to him, it sounds very bad on the whole, tho you say he was a shade better…offer to Henry for me to go up if he requires it- God bless you dearest.'[263] Henry died two days later, with William at his side. His epitaph was composed by author and fellow swindler Theodore Hook, and ran: 'Here lies the premier Baron of England, patiently awaiting the last trump'.

After Henry's death William and Georgy inherited the de Ros title and estates and William became the 23rd Baron de Ros. As the third son William had never expected to inherit and Georgy had married in the full knowledge that she was not going to take a title; yet now she held the oldest title in the country. The family moved to Cholmleys, a beautiful and expansive villa on the Thames Ditton estate, near Boyle Farm. This better fitted their new position, although William and Georgy chose to make their main residence Strangford Lough in Northern Ireland. In time they would rebuild the house there and call it Old Court. It became a much loved family home. The house was modest in comparison to other country estates in the area but had room for all the family and suited them perfectly. William and Georgy spent many a pleasant summers' day creating the pleasure gardens which surrounded the house, down to St. Catherine's Quay. They took an active interest in the lives of the Irish locals 'by whom they were much beloved.'[264] Money was still an issue as they had inherited large debts from Henry's addiction to gambling and resultant court costs. When they first inherited the estate there was talk that Georgy would be taken off the pension list which she received from the state in acknowledgment of her father's years of civic service. Queen Victoria wrote in her diary: 'Talked of the present Lord De Ros intending to give up Lady Georgiana's pension; "That's a flashy thing to do", said Lord M.' [265] As soon as William realised the true extent of Henry's debts however, it was clear that this was not going to be possible. Georgy remained on the pension list and when this was under threat, the ever-faithful Wellington petitioned the government on her behalf. He wrote to her on the subject in December 1837, teasing her for her political flexibility:

> 'Dearest Georgy, I was in hopes that the pension list would not be have been inquired into. The enquiry is infamous. As far as I can judge from what passed at the Debate, I think I struck the right Nail in your Letter, and that you are safe. Your being a Whig gives you a better chance, though the rascals know full well that you are not....'[266]

In the end Georgy was not taken off the pension list and Wellington congratulated her 'This Pension affair is like others- a mere Fallacy!'[267] The money Georgy received went to supporting the estates in Ireland and Ditton. However, life in Ireland was tremendously difficult at the time, as production was low and prices high. It was clear the de Ros family were living beyond their means and could not continue with both estates indefinitely.

26. Strangford, where Georgy and William spent many happy years together with their family.

Being happiest in Ireland, the de Ros family spent as much time there as possible. They did not receive many visitors from London, preferring to indulge in the simplicity of country life and to keep far away from the trappings of London life. The full calendar of social engagements which made up society there did not suit William's health either. Even Wellington found so much entertaining to be somewhat onerous at times. Asked constantly to sit for a portrait by every artist of merit, and many more without, the Duke complained to Georgy:

> 'Dearest Georgy, I did not write to ask you to come here when the Duke of Cambridge went away, as I expected a descent of artists. I have had one [possibly Sir George Hayter]; some still remain, and more are coming- two from Scotland. I literally lead the life of the subaltern officer of a regiment. I parade, dressed for duty, at nine in the morning, and again once or twice a day. There is not a moment of the day or night that I can call my own. These gentlemen are at my breakfast, dinner, and supper, and all the evening my existence is at their pleasure; I cannot move along the passage, or on the staircase, or the ramparts, without meeting them. Even I had [enough] rooms in the house for you and your family, which I have not, I could consider that I should make you as comfortable as I should wish to make a guest of mine by asking you to come here thus for my sins visited...'[268]

This characteristically grumpy letter is typical of the Duke as he was besieged by officials, politicians, society ladies and artists on a daily basis. Everyone wanted to see him, invite him to events and to have his opinion on matters of the day. Although he constantly complained that he never had enough time to do the things he most liked to do, namely relaxing at Walmer Castle with a few close friends, he believed he had a duty to both state and society. He would also have been appalled if he had not been invited to the major events of the day.

Despite his growing years the Duke's frame remained upright, his profile instantly recognisable. Regardless of the unpopular decisions he had made during his tenure as Prime Minister, he was still an undisputed national treasure. He wrote dozens of letters a day, answering even the most benign enquiry or entreaty in his famously sharp, clipped tone and more often than not in the third person. It was a welcome relief to receive Georgy's missives, long letters full of gossip about life in Ireland and stories about the children. As the children grew he was soon receiving letters from Fanny and Blanche too, who grew as fond of the Iron Duke as their mother was.

The Duke also shared with Georgy volumes of his official dispatches which had been compiled from official reports he had written during his campaigns in India, the Peninsular War and at Waterloo. This was a further mark of their close friendship and shared passion for reading and record-keeping. The reports are far from easy reading, yet Georgy poured over them with relish. They told her so much of the battles that she, being a young lady in society, would not and could not have known at the time. Georgy read many accounts, most unusual evening reading for a woman of that era. Wellington wrote to her 'I am glad you like the twelfth volume [of the Dispatches], it is curious, certainly.'[269] Wellington had been very reluctant to have his official reports published but had trusted his friend and private secretary John Gurwood to do the job. For military historians the dispatches are an invaluable source of information which span almost ten years of near-constant warfare across Europe. The publication of Wellington's military achievements through his dispatches coincides with his gradual retreat from public life. Although he remained in touch with London's political and social world, from the 1830's he began to actively seek a quieter life. After Kitty's death he found it was easier to receive friends at either Stratfield Saye or Walmer Castle. The Duke was an excellent host, always taking the time to individually escort each visitor to their room and show them around.

The Duke's health was also in decline. He suffered from rheumatism and was becoming increasingly deaf. He had a healthy distrust of doctors and maintained that the best thing to do when ill was to keep the body cold and to eat as little as possible. He once wrote to Georgy: 'The first thing of all is to get the Stomach right; and to keep it so by putting into it very little.'[270] His insistence on this starvation diet was a great worry to his friends who believed his methods to be extremely counter-productive. Despite his ill health, in March 1838 he wrote to Georgy that he was still taking an active role in reviews. He wrote: 'Dearest Georgy, I am sorry that the Queen did not come to my review on Wednesday. I took the battalion in hand myself, and knocked them about the Park, as I should have twenty-five years ago with an enemy in front, to their infinite amazement. I made them march in line, which they did beautifully, from Tyburn Gate to the statue of Achilles.'[271]

By autumn he was suffering again. From Stratfield Saye he wrote 'Dearest Georgy, I have been here about a week since my return from Kent, and I think that I continue to improve, but I am not yet quite comfortable on a horse's back. They advise me to go to Bath for eight or ten days longer, that is till the weather will be more settled.'[272] He wrote that Stratfield Saye, which had been undergoing modernising works to install central heating and flushing toilets totally ahead of its time, was finally finished. Impressed with the work, he reported that it was 'beautiful; I am myself astonished at the effect of the improvements.'[273] Despite his largely old-fashioned values, the Duke was surprisingly modern when it came to the comforts of his own home, something his guests particularly appreciated. Soon visitors to the house included a younger generation of women attracted to the Duke's charm and presence, very much still present despite his age. Harriet Arbuthnot had died and Marianne Patterson remarried, thus the position of Wellington's first lady was vacant; but this was not to be for long.

Wellington soon met a young lady called Miss Angela Burdett-Coutts who would soon entrance him more than any woman had done for years. Born the year before Waterloo, she was the daughter of the radical politician Sir Frances Burdett and her maternal grandfather was the famous banker Thomas Coutts. In 1837 she inherited her grandfather's vast fortune which amounted to some £1,800,000, making her the richest heiress in the country. Wellington wrote to Georgy after he first met Angela and her father, that he thought him 'a sensible Fellow!', but makes no mention of his beautiful daughter.[274] Angela was smart and serious, not given to flights of giddiness in his company as so many other young women were. She was quite capable of holding the Duke's attention on political matters despite the age gap between them. She was also a philanthropist and funded numerous charitable initiatives across the country, consulting the Duke on many occasions. This in turn appealed to his generous nature and social conscience. Before long Angela had fallen deeply in love with the Duke and for his part the Duke seemed equally smitten. They were seen out together regularly in London and in time she even had her own apartment at Stratfield Saye with an adjoining staircase to the Duke's quarters on the ground floor. When Angela was thirty-three and the Duke seventy-eight she proposed to him. Wellington was shocked and did not give her an answer but his written response the next day shows his deep and paternal affection for her:

> 'I have passed every Moment of the Evening and Night since I quitted you in reflecting upon our conversation of yesterday, Every Word of which I have considered repeatedly. My first Duty towards you is that of Friend, Guardian, Protector! You

> are Young, my Dearest! You have before you the prospect of at least twenty years of enjoyment and Happiness in Life. I entreat you again in this way, not to throw yourself away upon a Man old enough to be your Grandfather, who, however strong, Hearty and Healthy at present, must and will certainly in time feel the consequences and Infirmities of Age.'[275]

Despite refusing her hand in marriage, Angela and the Duke remained very close and saw each other regularly. The Duke had dealt with this potentially very awkward situation in a surprisingly tender and delicate way, preserving Angela's honour as well as their friendship. But Angela was not the only woman with whom Wellington had to contend in matters of the heart. A Miss Mary Ann Jervis, daughter of the Lord St. Vincent, was besotted with the Duke and soon earned herself the nickname 'The Syren'. Miss Jervis was a talented singer, dancer and composer, accomplishments which no doubt endeared her to the Duke and his circle of friends. She became a fashionable addition to many a party. Between the Duke and Georgy they often refer in their letters to 'The Musick' which is evidently a reference to Miss Jervis's musical and other less easily defined female talents.

Charles Arbuthnot wrote Georgy a letter which has survived in the de Ros archive, showing the strength of their friendship. It appears that having failed to win the affections of the Duke, Miss Jervis turned her charms on the widowed Artbuthnot. Trusting that 'what I may say shall go no further…' he confided in Georgy that Miss Jervis had:

> 'showered down upon me assurances without end of her great liking & admiration for me- that she had felt this from the very first and that in short her liking for me was risen only to that wch she had for the Duke. I assured her she was quite mistaken in fancying that there was anything in me to amuse

> or to interest, but it was all to no purpose as it was decided this with her that I was very charming. But you must always keep in mind that her fondness for me is only a stepping Stone for that which she feels for the Duke.'[276]

Arbuthnot then revealed an anecdote which he knew Georgy would enjoy. He had heard that on another occasion Miss Jervis and her friend Miss Ward had gone into the Duke's bedroom whilst he was out: 'They went into it, & when there Miss Jervis leant across and kissed the bed & then the Pillow, & seeing a Paper of Pins she seized it & dividing it in two she gave half to Miss Ward. Charging her to ever to keep it- & and put the other half into her breast. It was with great difficulty Miss Ward could get her out of the Room, dreading always that the Duke shd come and find her there...'[277] Although Wellington was undoubtedly very taken with his ravishing young beauty, this kind of embarrassing behaviour would have horrified him had he ever have discovered it. He once found Angela Burdett-Coutts in a similar situation in his private quarters and reprimanded her soundly: 'If you wish to see my Room and every Article it contains, I have no objection. Fix your hour regularly. Bring your friends with you. I will attend you. But do not be found here alone...In short I tell you very firmly I will not allow it.'[278] It was a form of hero-worshipping that he simply could not abide.

There is no denying that Miss Jervis and the Duke had become close over the years. Soon after Kitty's death the Duke had given her, in her musical role as 'Queen of Music', a gold crown with his initial 'W' encrusted with diamonds, which he had commissioned from a top London jeweller.[279] On other occasions she received gifts such an octagonal pianoforte and several pieces of jewellery such as 'a Ducal

Coronet in small diamonds, with the Duke of Wellington's hair at the back'.[280] We know from Wellington's relationship with Georgy and his other female companions that he loved to give expensive gifts. These presents, although lavish, are not necessarily indicative of any extra physical dimension to his relationship with Miss Jervis. However, they are telling, and the Duke was clearly more enthralled by Miss Jervis and her beautiful singing voice than he was letting on to Georgy or any of his other friends. 'The Syren' came to London and the Duke wrote to Georgy, 'I have not seen her or heard from her. Lady L de Horsey told me that she was come.'[281] Despite this Georgy found out that the two had met at Lady Salisbury's and Wellington admitted 'She was looking in great force; and says that she is much improved in Musick.'[282]

A few months later Wellington and Miss Jervis dined together. Wellington promised Georgy 'I have not met her since. I hope that I shall not get into any Scrape to render necessary my giving a retainer to the great lawyers in such Cases.'[283] The Duke had never got himself into such a position before. His expensive gifts to Miss Jervis had clearly been misinterpreted and whilst she saw the potential for marital bliss, his thoughts could not have been further from this. In an interesting role reversal, he sought counsel from Georgy as it was now he that required advice on how to proceed in matters of the heart. In the past it had been Georgy's courtships that required the Duke's opinion but she was now more than happy to give her thoughts on the matter. Clearly the Duke did not intend to marry Miss Jervis although he seemed unable to distance himself from her attentions satisfactorily. He admitted to Georgy that 'I quite approve of her object but not her judgement in the choice of her mode of preceding,'[284] for her behaviour was becoming more unbecoming and erratic the more she attempted to pin the Duke down on the matter. She wrote passionately in her diary:

> 'I cannot be lukewarm about such a man as the Duke...for nobody scarcely can feel and understand what he is. The generality of the world contemplate him as the ablest of the politicians and the most glorious of warriors, and so he is; arrayed in the wisdom of Solomon and crowned with the glory of Caesar, but this they cannot comprehend, that he is to be loved, almost adored, admired, venerated besides which no other mortal man could ever have merited in like degree.'[285]

This remarkable admission of her feelings clearly illustrates the unsuitability of the Duke and Miss Jervis as a couple. The Duke could not stand women who fawned over his celebrity and such flowery sentiment was not in keeping with his image of the ideal Duchess. As the years progressed the Duke tried to distance himself from Miss Jervis but was only partially successful in doing so. Soon a new rumour flew about that Miss Jervis was to marry Lord Lowther, which Georgy asked the Duke about. The Duke replied to her 'Dearest Georgy, I should like to see the Syren married to Lord Lowther or anybody excepting myself. God bless her! I cannot conceive how she came to think of me. I am old enough to be her Great Grandfather!'[285a] Despite this admission the next month Miss Jervis remained a main subject of conversation. This time it was reported that Miss Jervis and the Duke had secretly married, prompting another letter from Georgy. Wellington replied 'I had not heard of my new Bride. There can be no foundation for the Report, for she is not mad!!!,[286] implying that Georgy was.

Things came to a head that October when Miss Jervis sent the Duke another letter requesting a visit. He forwarded this letter on to Georgy, again illustrating their closeness and the value he placed on her opinion and advice: 'I conclude that I must receive this visit', he wrote, 'I do not know how I am to decline, particularly as I shall have people there. Send back this note by tomorrows post.'[287] The Duke begged Georgy 'Pray do not say anything about this Affair or its Result. The only mischief of it consists in the Gossip which it creates.'[288] Beseeching Georgy to hold her tongue, knowing how much she loved to gossip, indicates how serious the situation was. It appears that Miss Jervis's intention was marriage. The Duke managed to carefully manoeuvre the situation so as not to cause any offence to her or her father Lord St. Vincent. Luckily for him, in the end Miss Jervis 'behaved very properly.'[289]

It was 1840 when Miss Jervis finally married, and it was thankfully not to Wellington but to a Mr David Dyce Sombre; whose story is a fascinating one worthy of inclusion here. Sombre was the Anglo-Indian stepson and heir to the famous Begum Sumra who ruled over a small principality just north of Delhi. When she died in 1836 the East India Company seized Sombre's newly inherited kingdom, refusing to recognise him as the Begum's rightful heir. Sombre was forced to flee to England to fight his claim where he met Miss Jervis and later married her. Having secured his marriage to the daughter of a Viscount, his position was further strengthened by his election as an MP in 1841. He was the first Anglo-Indian to achieve such a status. However, the following year his life collapsed when the election was annulled under claims of corruption. His marriage fell apart, Miss Jervis's family declared him insane and took his considerable fortune for their own. Sombre managed to escape the lunatic asylum to which he had been sent and lived in exile in France. He loudly professed his innocence and sanity and tried to reclaim his fortune from his estranged wife, sadly dying before this could be achieved.

Sombre was very unpopular within polite society, with Wellington's circle of friends finding his over-the-top displays of wealth unseemly. Having been brought up in an idiosyncratic Indian court his customs and manners were unfamiliar and strange to those he met in the salons and concert halls of London. No doubt he did suffer with his mental health, possibly the result of a sexual illness, but he was also treated very cruelly by a society he thought would accept him as one of their own. Georgy and the Duke called Mr Sombre 'The Black Prince'. The Duke wrote to Georgy from Stratfield Saye after news of Miss Jervis' engagement had been announced 'I had heard of the Bagums dissatisfaction with the Black Prince. [If] She [Miss Jervis] is not more discreet in her choice of confidantes, than she has shown herself in that of a husband. The story if well known. I don't know what we are to do for Musick next year...All the wicked are behaving as well as they can.'[290] The Duke, who still cared for Miss Jervis, did not approve of her choice in husband, a judgement which proved to be correct in time. Slowly Miss Jervis slipped away from their social circle, leaving Wellington to enjoy the company of his female friends who created less drama.

In February 1840 Wellington wrote 'Dearest Georgy, I am much obliged to you for the letter which I received this morning. I am invited to be present in St. James's Chapel at the wedding.'[291] The wedding was to be that of Queen Victoria to Prince Albert of Saxe-Coburg and Gotha. Georgy knew the Queen fairly well and on occasion would go to the Palace for tea. William and Albert got to know each other professionally over the coming years and in 1852 Georgy's son Dudley would become the Prince's equerry. Wellington continued 'I am quite well indeed as well as I ever have been. I hope so to keep myself. I was on Horseback at S.S. for several hours on Friday and again yesterday. Please God I will be at the Death of a fox or two before the close of the Season; and then the Common Enemy will begin to believe in the continued existence of my Iron Hand.'[292] Old age was approaching and the Duke was conscious of his growing infirmity. One way of proving he was still strong was out on the hunting field. He hunted every season, whatever the weather, and quite terrified his friends and family with the number of risks he took. After having suffered his first stroke the previous year, he suffered several epileptic fits in 1847, perhaps as a result of how far he pushed himself.

Meanwhile trouble was brewing for Wellington's eldest son Douro. Although a favourable match had been made with the lovely Elizabeth Hay, it appears that Douro would not settle and confirm his engagement to her. Wellington wrote to Georgy:

> 'I find that I am like KG4th [King George IV]. He had a Daughter to be Married [Princess Charlotte] and he had arranged with her for the Choice of a Son in Law [The Prince of Orange]. But she had other Lovers; and he told me one morning that instead of having one Son in Law as he imagined he found that he had three! In a like manner I have a marriageable son; but instead of having one Daughter in Law I am to have I don't know how many, of all Ranks and Religions, most of them however I believe without any at all of the latter...'[293]

In his next letter he grumbled 'I believe you have as much chance of a Daughter in Law as I have,'[294] as Dudley Fitzgerald-de Ros was no closer to choosing a wife than Douro was. When Georgy enquired after the Duke's sons he replied rather tersely 'I don't know anything about either of my sons! But I consider them the foolishest fellows going about.'[295]

In the end the marriage between Douro and Elizabeth did take place but it was not a happy union. To her great distress, Elizabeth was unable to bear children and was often very unwell. Somewhat surprisingly given his fraught relations with Douro, the Duke took a shine to Elizabeth and doted on her entirely. Priscilla Burghersh in one of her charming letters to Georgy recalled the Duke's comment to Queen Victoria after they had all attended the christening of the Princess Royal together in February 1841:

> 'he told the Queen how much he admired the Baby & his speech was- "It's the nicest Baby I ever saw & I wish to God Lady Douro had done her Business as well as yr Majesty." He told it to me the next morning, & I am sure correctly, for having since dined at the Palace, the Queen asked me if the Duke had told me how much he admired the Baby & then she repeated his speech word for word- seeming highly pleased with it. Poor Ly Douro! My hopes for her are [that] she certainly is in very bad health & therefore if that gets right she may yet do her business but in the meantime she is quite miserable about it- has lost all her spirits & is always fretting; she is much thinner & paler than last year but still very handsome. She is a very amiable & interesting Creature & the Duke is very fond of her.'[296]

This comment to the Queen about Lady Douro doing 'her business' may seem heartless but securing the line of succession was of supreme importance to Wellington. The Duke cared very deeply for Lady Douro and wanted her to be happy but having produced two sons himself, it was a great disappointment not to see Douro and Elizabeth provide an heir. Georgy later recorded in her diary of the Duke's relationship with Lady Douro 'The Duke is so kind to her, always thinking of her making her happy and comfortable and loading her with presents.'[297] All eyes were on Elizabeth to bring a pregnancy to term and this pressure must have added to her great distress at being unable to do so. It was some consolation that the Duke's second son Charles had made a satisfactory marriage to Augusta Sophia Pierrepoint and went on to have six children, with two of their children becoming the 3rd and 4th Dukes of Wellington respectively.

CHAPTER ELEVEN

Remembrance

'It seems as if it would alter one's existence. The world without that great name, one can hardly believe it!'[298]

Lady Georgina Bathurst to Georgiana Lady de Ros

The Duke was not at all well although he kept the severity of the situation away from his friends as much as he could. So in 1840 Georgy decided that in order to get a full and faithful report of his health she would engage the Duke's valet Kendall in correspondence. It is likely that if Wellington had known about this, he would not have approved. Kendall now wrote to Georgy:

> 'I am sorry to inform Your Ladyship that the Duke has been attacked again with his complaint...he was from last Night till eleven quite insensible having a strong fit every five Minutes, the Doctor saying the next fit would take him off. I am happy to say he slept at intervals in the Night and appears better in

the morning. Very week quite sensible, he appears to have lost the use of his left side...'[299]

Luckily the Duke rallied and Kendall wrote 'I am happy to inform Your Ladyship the Duke is going on well he had a good Night and is at Business this Morning he is quite out of immediate danger he has not yet been out he is still very weak and thin.'[300] The doctors reported that Wellington was now much improved.

The following year was also punctuated by further reports of the Duke's illness. He had an attack during a sitting of the House of Lords, about which Priscilla Burghersh wrote to Georgy: 'I am happy to be able now to say that he really is as well as before his last attack- He has within the last week resumed his usual habits- but I think he is more careful of himself- & that the circumstance of his attack having come on in the House of Lords makes him feel the necessity of care more than he Ever did before.' She added that 'he has been very much annoyed at it & is still in bad spirits,'[301] knowing that his infirmity was now common knowledge. The Duke continued to attend the House of Lords and other official duties, although as he had become largely deaf he hated large parties for the noise disturbed and annoyed him. However small gatherings at Stratfield Saye and Walmer Castle still brought him much joy and over the coming years he continued to receive visits from the de Ros family and other friends. He particularly loved spending time with his many grandchildren and god-children. In 1847 the whole de Ros family went to Stratfield Saye for Easter. Georgy recorded in her diary: 'the Douro's, Mahon's and Lord Strangford here. The Duke extremely well and amused with Blanche's singing,'[302] Later on during the same trip she wrote 'Blanche played and sang, the Duke delighted, just as kind and good-natured as ever.'[303]

Georgy often recorded these little details in her diary, delighting in the love that her oldest friend had for her children.

Fanny and Dudley were now young adults. Dudley was a hard-working and thoughtful young man who had recently purchased a sub-lieutenancy in the Life Guards, the same regiment as his father. Fanny had grown into a beautiful young woman with dark hair and features similar to her mother. She attended many balls in London where she saw the Duke. She recorded in one letter to her mother of her conversation with him, 'I believe we were almost the only people he knew in the room there. He was so nice about you & Dudley… He shook hands with me & asked me how "the boy" [Dudley] was, directly we were near enough to him & went on talking to Papa for a considerable time.'[304] The Duke was in turn very fond of Fanny whom he gave the nickname 'Mildred'. He continued to be the centre of attention wherever he went and would have delighted in seeing a familiar face, such a Fanny's, in amongst the crowds of those just wanting to get a glimpse of him. Fanny reported to her mother at one such event, that 'the Duke had given 'a résumé of the whole war, in a most humorous & interesting manner…The Duke brought Papa to me with him, & talked over the Debate [in the House of Lords] with him, entering into all the military details in a most interesting way. He was in very high force & very novel spirits & Papa, of course was amused.'[305] Although she loved being out and socialising, Fanny was often plagued by various illnesses, not named in correspondence at the time, and was therefore a regular source of concern to her parents.

On one occasion when Dudley had also fallen ill and Georgy had been tending to him, she wrote to William from Apsley House 'I enjoyed my dinner much for the Duke was so kind.' He said to her at dinner 'I thought it would do you good to come away from your boy's sick-bed, and as he is doing so well, I thought I would send after you.'[306] At this large dinner Georgy was pleased to be seated next to Wellington, just like she had in Brussels, even though this place of honour was no longer her privilege.

Georgy's task was now to guide her own daughters through the excitements of London's social scene in the same way that her mother and Lady Bathurst had supported her. Sadly, these figureheads of the previous generation were beginning to slip away and with them the traditions and formalities of a society which they had gracefully dominated. In 1841 Georgy's beloved aunt Lady Bathurst passed away whilst the de Ros family were holidaying in Marseilles. It was some months before Georgy was able to pen a note to her mother 'I have left your kind letter so long unanswered but my grief at poor dear Lady Bathurst's death made my quite ill, & I suffered much from a succession of bad nervous headaches, you know how devotedly attached to her I was, & therefore you will easily believe what a blow it was to me.'[307] The following year the Dowager Duchess herself passed away. No letters about this have survived but Georgy must have been devastated to lose not one but two of her greatest female role models in such quick succession. Although the two women were very different in character they had both played an essential part in Georgy's upbringing. They were also the last links to the eighteenth century and all its values, which was already becoming a bygone age.

Georgy inherited from her mother several pieces of jewellery including diamond earrings, a golden chain with a lock of her father's hair and various personal possessions which had more sentimental than financial significance. William was personally bequeathed a print of the

Duke of York and a secretaire writing desk with a marble top. In fact, the Duchess of Richmond's legacy would prove to be a lasting one as it was her Gordon blood that finally saved the Lennoxes from permanent financial ruin. For over three generations the Richmonds had struggled against debt that threatened to banish them from the way of life they had helped to establish. However, when in 1836 the 5th and last Duke of Gordon, Charlotte's brother, died with no legitimate heir, Charlotte inherited her family's vast fortune. In 1842 this money passed to Georgy's brother the 5th Duke of Richmond who took on the additional name of Gordon in honour of his mother's heritage, a tradition which continues to this day. So after a turbulent marriage with Charlotte's excessive gambling debts contributing to the Lennoxes lifelong financial worries, it was actually her money that saved the Richmond dynasty from ruin. Georgy and her brother remained on good terms, she continued to refer fondly to him as March; and he would send the de Ros family braces of pheasant from the Goodwood estate.

1851 was a year of note for the nation, as with it came the Great Exhibition, which brought together fascinating objects of industry from all corners of the Empire. For the de Ros family however, tragedy was again on the doorstep. The family had been residing mostly in Ireland as life was cheaper there and money was still a concern. Charlotte's money may have saved Georgy's brother but none made its way to save the de Ros incumbents. The family's debts were increasing as the estate struggled to break even alongside the political and social difficulties in Ireland at the time. But soon these concerns were pushed aside as Fanny became ill once again. The family returned to London where they could be near the best medical advice and where the case was confirmed as tuberculosis. Over the years Fanny's body had been weakened by prolonged bouts of illness which had taken their toll. Although it seemed at first that she would again pull through, this time it was not to be. She was only twenty-six. William reported to family friend Edward Campbell:

> 'On the 14th we perceived a little undoing of the mind which gradually increased to unconsciousness, but never with the smallest excitement or distress. She mumbled about her innocent pursuits & amusements talked of her friends naming you & many others as connected with our residence in Cholmleys in past years & in short appeared to live in an agreeable dream. But alas in the meantime her strength rapidly decreased & though the fever almost ceased on the 20th it left her without power to rally & to conclude this sad sad story she breathed her last on the 21st with a peace & calmness so like the sleep of a child that her mother did not at first perceive it was all over...'[308]

Her illness had been quiet, free 'from suffering, of mind or body' which enabled 'her dear Mother & Blanche to find full relief in tears & to exert themselves for mutual support.'[309] The loss of Fanny was devastating and Georgy, like any grieving mother, would never fully recover. There are no letters from Georgy during the family's period of deep mourning and it can only be assumed that such was her suffering, she was in no fit state to write. William wrote that 'grief has weighed down upon her so heavily, [so] that I really feared until lately that her health & spirit would give way together.'[310]

With Fanny's death the family retreated to quietly mourn her and there are some poignant examples of this which the family preserved in their archive. Edward Campbell replied to William '...I am so glad Lady de

Ros & Blanche have not given way under the blows for it was a hard one- When Dudley comes and they are able to talk it quietly over they will be much more comforted for you cant look back on Fanny's life without remembering how good gentle, kind hearted and pure she was.'[311] At the time of Fanny's death, Dudley was in the Mediterranean with the Army but arranged to return home directly. He had taken the loss of his sister very badly and was reduced to an extremely anxious state. The rest of the family retreated to Aix le Chapelle to mourn and to take the waters but Dudley had to return to his military duties. Blanche wrote 'we were also obliged to leave dear poor Dudley in London. Poor boy, the terribly sudden way in which he heard he had lost his darling sister, took such an effect upon his nerves that he was in a dreadfully nervous state for a long time.'[312] Contrary to the image of Victorian reserve in such matters, these letters indicate the real emotional distress the family were going through.

As life slowly returned to normal William and Georgy were forced to frankly assess their situation in Ireland and make some drastic changes. Their sustained financial problems had put an even greater strain on Georgy's mental and physical health. The Duke, ever conscious of ways he could practically help the family, offered William a new position which would greatly add to his meagre earnings as a Colonel. Through his position as Constable of the Tower of London Wellington offered him the position of Deputy Lieutenant of the Tower. Georgy recorded in her diary 'William to House of Lords, where the Duke in a most amiable manner, offered him to be Deputy Lieutenant of the Tower, a very agreeable office, it will increase our income and we shall have much more liberty-it is to be a secret at the moment.'[313] This further shows the Duke's kindness and attention in always helping them in practical ways. Despite his physical decline, he was still a man of action, quick to help those he cared about most.

A few days later more good news arrived. Georgy wrote 'William got a letter from Lord Derby [the Prime Minister] offering him to be Captain of the Yeoman of the Guard, he went to the Duke to consult him whether it would embarrass Lord Derby his having just got the Tower appointment.'[314] Evidently the Duke did not believe there was a conflict of interest as William gratefully accepted both posts. It would prove to be a huge financial relief to the family and allowed Georgy to regain some of her old sparkle. William wrote 'I think too that the change for the better in our circumstances which, even if I hold my last office but 6 months, will nearly clear us of debt which had most reluctantly incurred during the severity of the distress in Ireland has had its effect in removing an annoyance from her [Georgy's] mind.'[314a]

Georgy and William were sorry to leave Ireland but gratefully accepted the turn in their fortunes. William continued 'I am sorry to give up my Country but the Duke offered me the Tower so kindly & so entirely unasked, & the income of it is so much more (about double that of Major) that I could not have refused it...My other appointment, the Yeoman of the Guard, as little solicited & quite as little expected as the Tower, is as good & better indeed than the Tower.'[315] The family relocated to London and took a house in Cadogan Place so William could be near his places of work.

For some years Chomleys had been a financial strain on the family so they now endeavoured to sell it. William wrote 'I had a great fondness for that place, but it certainly was beyond our fixed income & neither Dudley nor Blanche ever liked it much, nor could we see so much of the Duke who is such a comfort to them & to me anywhere as in London, though certainly to live there much does not suit my health.'[316] When they finally sold the property in 1852 William reflected on its 'fine court & those happy scenes of former merriment & happiness',[317] but for Georgy it was no great loss as she had always felt more at home in Strangford. William hoped that they would now be able to spend some four or five months of the year at Strangford but for the time being they must remain in London. That summer the family enjoyed seeing more of the Duke of Wellington. Georgy recorded 'We went to the Tower to receive the Duke...Poor Blanche could not go on account of her cold. The Duke sent her a bouquet.'[318] A few days later it was Blanche's birthday and the Duke gave Blanche a 'very pretty present' of a diamond and opal brooch.[319]

Meanwhile the Great Exhibition had started and had become a huge success with crowds of people flooding the Crystal Palace every day. Wellington visited several times, finding the collection of objects from the around the world completely fascinating. He attracted as much attention as the exhibits themselves and would often be seen with a trail of people following him. One of the most spectacular exhibits was the Koh-i-Noor diamond which had recently come into the possession of Queen Victoria after the British defeat of the Punjab in 1849. The stone had been fought over since its discovery in the thirteenth century and supposedly had mystical powers and the ability to curse any male ruler who wore it. Wellington was present with Prince Albert when the stone was recut in July 1852, leaving it the brilliant jewel it is today, to be seen on the Queen Mother's Crown and on display at the Tower of London.

For those that saw him at the exhibition, it was clear that Wellington was now nearing the end of his life. He enjoyed one more peaceful Christmas and spring surrounded by numerous grandchildren, great nephews, nieces, and godchildren. Towards the summer of 1852 he became increasingly weak and he died that September at Walmer Castle surrounded by family, including his younger son Lord Charles and his wife. It was a fitting end for the Duke to die in a place he loved so much. He had reached the respectable age of eighty-three years old and his passing was free from drawn out suffering.

Although they had known that the Duke had been in ill-health for some years, it was still a huge shock for Georgy and her family to hear the news of his death. The last months they had spent in London where they had seen the Duke were a lasting comfort to them. Georgy was in London when she received a letter from Kendall, Wellington's valet. It ran 'My Lady, It is my painful duty to inform you that the Duke of Wellington departed this life this day at ¼ past three o'clock after a few hours illness. I will write more fully by the next post.'[320] Another letter was sent the same day in case the first had not reached her:

> 'I sent a letter this afternoon by messenger to your House in London but should you be at Strangford possibly you may receive this first. It is my painful duty to inform you that the Duke of Wellington Died this Afternoon at a ¼ past three o'clock. He was as well as usual yesterday and went to Bed to all appearances quite well. I found him unwell this morn when I went to his Room but capable of asking me to send for the Doctor he gradually got worse and Died in the time above stated. Lord and Lady Charles are in the Castle and witnessed his last.'[321]

Georgy recorded in her diary 'Alas alas the fatal news of the dear

Duke's death reached us this morning he died at Walmer Castle on the 14th having been ill for a few hours. Thank God! he did not suffer but oh what a loss to the world! From childhood I loved and venerated him and invariably received the most unremitting kindness from him and so many years of unclouded friendship cannot be given up without much suffering.'[322] William wrote 'G much affected; & indeed we never had a more steady & true friend, nor one who took more concern in our welfare & more interest in our distresses and afflictions.'[323] It was another personal blow to Georgy and the end of an era for the rest of the country which fell into a period of public mourning. The Duke had been a giant, a titan of Victorian society. His absence from it sent shockwaves across the country.

Lord Douro, who now succeeded his father to the many titles and honours that had been bestowed upon his father between 1806 and 1815, is said to have remarked 'Imagine what it will be when the Duke of Wellington is announced, and only I walk in the room'. Living up to the name of his father having walked for so long in his shadow was not going to be easy. William wrote a letter of condolence to Douro who often referred to himself as such despite now being the 2nd Duke of Wellington. Douro's rather touching reply to William ran 'I don't wonder at people making themselves callous to the death of others, the pain is too dreadful. Things that one cannot account for gives ones tears...When a little time has passed you must come and choose some relic of your friend.'[324] Far from choosing a showy or valuable object they chose a rather ordinary pair of scissors which apparently had lain on the Duke's writing table for the duration of their long friendship. This underlines that personal and private grief that both Georgy and William felt by the absence of their greatest friend.

Further examples of private remembrances of the Duke and his life were shared between the de Ros family and friends who had also known him well. These intimate letters showed how close they all were to the man himself and how deeply they felt the loss of him. Priscilla Burghersh wrote to Georgy from Vienna:

> 'The remembrance of those happy days at Walmer bring the same agonising reflections to me...I have suffered so much since that time & seen so many fond hopes cut short, that I did not think anything cd ever again affect me as deeply as the loss of my dear Uncle has done- Indeed it is very bitter to me who have for 40 years ever found in him the kindest & most affectionate Friend- & never more so than in these last sad years to me. And though his great age ought to have prepared me at any time to lose him the blow came so suddenly! I was expecting him at Dover where he had promised to come & pass the day with me on my way to Calais- When I heard that he was ill I hastened to Walmer, I arrived there a quarter of an hour after he had expired. It is a consoling reflection to me since, that I was able to take a last farewell & kiss his dear face before any change over it & certainly for him one should not lament so easy a termination after so long a life!'[325]

Lady Georgina Bathurst wrote to Georgy to report that Queen Victoria who was also deeply affected by the loss of the Duke had written a 'really beautiful' note calling the Duke 'the greatest patriot, and the most devoted servant to the Crown this country ever had'. Georgina could 'hardly believe he is here no longer to be referred to... The Duchess of Cambridge shed many tears in talking of the Duke, but feels, as we all must, that we ought to be thankful he was taken before his faculties failed.'[326]

Contrary to the private reactions to Wellington's death illustrated by the intimate writings of Georgy and her friends, there was the very grandiose form of public Victorian mourning which the nation embraced with macabre relish. Plans were quickly drawn up for a state funeral the scale of which would have been befitting a member of the Royal Family. Objects and tokens adorned with the Duke's image were on sale within days of his death. Georgy did not partake in any of the rituals that followed in the coming weeks, her health was bad and she preferred to mourn the loss of Wellington privately in Ireland. William however, was in London, and was to play an important role in the proceedings.

The Duke's body was laid in state at Walmer Castle and thousands of local people filed past the dimly lit open coffin. On 10th November the coffin was transported to London by railway, where for a week the Duke was laid in state at Chelsea Hospital. The hall was elaborately draped in black cloth and was lit by fifty-four huge candles placed in holders seven feet high. The scene was extraordinarily macabre. Members of the Royal Family, the extended Wellington family and aristocracy visited on the first two days. Georgina Bathurst attended and wrote to Georgy 'To my mind the room in black cloth, with soldiers on each side with arms reversed, was very sad and appropriate. The intense crowd was wonderful, and so it will be on the day.'[326a] referring to the state funeral which was to be the largest and most elaborate spectacle seen by that generation.

Over the next few days such was the public outpouring of grief that tens of thousands of people came from far and wide to view the body of the Duke of Wellington. Such vast numbers had not been expected and before long order gave way to shoving and pushing. Three people were suffocated and several other seriously injured. Despite this some

50,000 people managed to pass through the hall on this first day. By the time it was shut a more manageable system had been put in place by the Army and some 235,000 people had managed to see the Duke before he was finally laid to rest.

William was chosen to lead the logistical organisation on the day of the funeral, an honour of which he was extremely proud. He wrote:

> 'I am quite touched by this act of kindness of Lord Hardinge. He took me aside (at Lord Derby's dinner), and he said he knew no one who has more veneration for the Duke's memory; and thinking it would be agreeable to my feelings to take an active part in the rendering him the last honours, he had put me in orders as Quartermaster-General of the troops assembled for the occasion, under command of H.R.H. the Duke of Cambridge.'[327]

William was tasked with organising the military procession of around 100,000 men which would progress the two miles from Horse Guards, past Buckingham Palace and down Piccadilly, then across the Strand to complete the journey at St. Paul's Cathedral. This was to be the Duke's final and fitting resting place. It was a colossal undertaking and William soon found the days in the run up to the funeral were filled with meetings, orders and rehearsals.

The funeral itself took place on a cold and bleak day in November 1852. All those involved with staging this massive spectacle, including the Duke of Cambridge and Prince Albert, had worked tirelessly to bring representatives from all areas of the Duke's public life together. For William this was the pinnacle of his public military life, despite it taking place on the streets of Victorian London not the battlefields of

Europe. The procession included 'two regiments of the line, a battalion of the royal marines, the household troops, cavalry and infantry, representatives of every regiment or other corps in the British Army', as well 'representatives of all the great authorities, including the ministers of state, Prince Albert, and generals or princes from foreign courts.'[328] William afterwards reflected 'In the narrow streets no troops in the world could have done it better- all out of zeal and obedience.'[329]

After weeks of preparation the day's event finally began and the procession moved off. The band from each regiment played the Death March from Handel's Saul. The buildings that the procession passed were draped in black, as were the stands that had been erected to accommodate the vast number of people who had purchased a ticket to view the spectacle. The spectators also wore black and everyone watched in silent solemnity. Queen Victoria and her children watched the procession from the balcony of Buckingham Palace before travelling to St. James's Palace to see it again. Women were not included in the parade, as it was not deemed appropriate, so close female friends and family watched from Apsley House, each saying their final goodbyes to the Duke. The day was not without its dramas. At a crucial moment William discovered the Lord Mayor had stopped his carriage exactly where a regiment was supposed to form into line and process forward. So William ordered twenty men to pick up the carriage and physically move both coach and occupant out of the way, just in time.

The main focus of the procession was the funeral car itself. It was designed to Prince Albert's exact specifications and was festooned with symbols of Wellington's many victories. Craftsmen laboured night and day for three weeks to finish this colossal structure which was twenty-seven feet long, ten feet wide and weighed ten tons. It required twelve of the strongest dray horses to pull it which were borrowed from a local brewery. Every surface of the structure was covered in trophies, pieces of artillery, field-marshal batons and cannon balls. The coffin perched on top was draped in silk and silver and looked entirely diminutive on top of its vast base. Georgina Bathurst wrote to Georgy 'We are returned from seeing the sad procession from Gloucester House. As far as there all went well; it was a melancholy and striking sight, but the car! Oh, so frightful! I can't describe it. I must leave it to the Morning Post.'[330] Greville reported that the procession was a 'Rather fine sight, and all well done, except the Car, which was tawdy, cumbrous & vulgar.'[331] The funeral car was so heavy that it got stuck on the Mall and William was forced to send for a police sergeant to control the situation, whilst ordering thirty Life Guards and forty Foot Guards to drag the funeral car out of its rut and escort it to safer position. All this took place whilst the service was underway in St. Paul's Cathedral but they managed to get the car moved just before the service ended. Inside the cathedral all natural light was blocked out and instead the sombre interior was lit with 6,000 gas jets. As Wellington was finally laid to rest, psalms were sung to music composed by the Duke's father, Lord Mornington.

After the funeral day was finally over William was able to reflect that despite this being a very public display of mourning, it had also provided a personal comfort, 'a sort of obligation to his memory and a relief to many painful thoughts.'[332] No doubt also referring to the loss of his daughter, organising the funeral had been a cathartic process for his own personal grief. He continued:

> 'At length this heavy load is off my back. Yesterday I was nearly eleven hours on my unfortunate horse. However,

> everybody tells me that the march and formation of the troops was perfectly managed. It was at the stroke of eight that the first section moved off, and in exactly four hours the whole infantry was formed, and the cavalry and guns packed away in back streets, with a clear passage for the car and carriages, but the anxiety and fatigue were great. The Duke of Cambridge thanked me in the most friendly, cordial way, when we parted at 5.30, after all was over.'[333]

A few days later a letter arrived from St. James's Palace, written by the Duke of Cambridge. It ran 'I cannot deprive myself of the pleasure of again assuring you that I am extremely indebted to you for the trouble you took in aiding my humble endeavours that all should go well on the occasion of so great and so national a solemnity.'[334] William was finally free to return to Strangford where he found Georgy a little better than he left her but still confined to her couch and garden chair.

The death of the Duke took yet another toll on Georgy's health. She had known and loved him for so long and he had been the one constant in her life through all her achievements and losses. Undoubtedly she loved him as truly as she had her father and as she did William. If he had not been married when they met Georgy certainly would have been in line to become the Duke's perfect Duchess, but somehow the fact their relationship was not physical made it more special; and no doubt made it last longer. This gave her an edge over the many of women who flocked to Wellington's bed during those heady days at Waterloo and Cambrai. Her relationship with him had stood the test of time because their caring feelings for each other went beyond that of lust and longing. The Duke once said 'no woman ever loved me: never in my whole life.'[335] Such self-deprecation was one of the Duke's most charming characteristics, but he must have known in Georgy's case that this was not true.

The nation's mourning was deep and heart-felt and also signified the loss not just of an individual but of an entire way of life which Wellington had fought to defend and protect. Indeed, the world had changed so very much since he had entered it eighty-three years previously. At least three generations had never known an England without its Great Duke of Wellington. He was a universal symbol for England, its Victorian principles and for peace. The Duke's funeral has come to symbolise for many the kind of mass hysteria associated with the Victorian's obsession with death and pageantry. In their grandiose commemoration of Wellington the man, they were also celebrating their own social ideals of service, duty and solemnity. Wellington had become the embodiment of that Victorian tradition, but for so many of the people who actually witnessed the event, it was simply the best way they could say goodbye to the man they loved. Many more, Georgy included, mourned privately and away from the crowds, readjusting to life without the Great Duke.

CHAPTER TWELVE

Reminiscences

'It is impossible to realise that you are 94; we feel you as young as ourselves, and more full of life and energy than many of us.'[336]

A birthday congratulation from a great-niece to the Dowager Lady de Ros, 1889

A year after the Duke's funeral there was some good news at last – a marriage celebration. Dudley had finally decided to settle down and marry Lady Elizabeth Egerton, daughter of the 2nd Earl of Wilton. The ceremony took place on 12th October 1853 and Georgy was delighted. The couple would go on to have one daughter, Mary, who would later inherit the title of Baroness de Ros. In 1865 Blanche also made a happy marriage to the well-respected painter James Rannie Swinton who was one of the many popular portrait artists of the day. Included in the long list of works completed by him are beautiful portraits of the 2nd Duchess of Wellington, who remained a friend of the de Ros family for many years. Blanche did not have any children but remained a constant companion to Georgy as she entered her golden years. Swinton painted a portrait of Georgy shortly after his marriage to Blanche, depicting her in a lace shawl and bonnet with a black neck choker, her hands resting elegantly on the sewing basket on her lap. Fortunately, the portrait was engraved as the original has since been lost. Swinton had first exhibited at the Royal Academy's Summer Exhibition in 1844 and remained a regular contributor there for the next thirty years. Blanche and Georgy took great delight in visiting the exhibition and peering up at his works on the walls.

In 1854 William and Georgy endured another separation when he served as Quartermaster- General in Turkey during the Crimea War. This time Georgy's worst fears came true when William contracted a deadly disease called Varna fever and very nearly died. Reports later said that the fever had been the result of William's rather eccentric passion for sunbathing, something he is said to have popularised. Whatever the cause of the fever he was unable to continue with his military duties and was sent back to Old Court where his recuperation was monitored closely by Georgy and Blanche. Thereafter William's health would always be troubling, with periodic relapses of the Varna fever; but each time he rallied and returned to health. Over the next quiet years of retirement Georgy enjoyed spending as much time with her family as possible and she and William were each other's constant companions.

As the years passed the family settled into life without the Duke and without their regular visits to Stratfield Saye and Walmer Castle. William and Georgy spent the seasons together between Old Court and London and enjoyed two winters in Cannes. In the summer months several of William's yachting friends would come to stay at Old Court, anchoring at St. Catherine's Quay. Georgy was very popular with the locals with whom she always made an enormous effort, organising picnics and boating parties. One young visitor at the time recalled Georgy's fame within the small Irish community there:

> 'It would be impossible to enumerate her many acts of kind thoughtfulness to the poor in her village, where 'her Ladyship's' visits were greatly welcomed and valued. This kindness was equally shown to all who came to the house. The young people of the neighbourhood, who used to meet at Old Court for picnics, boating-parties, croquet, etc., felt the keen interest taken by Lady de Ros in all that went on. In the winter amusements, charades, etc., which used to take place at Old Court, she would enter heartily into all the preparations, sparing no pains or trouble to make all go off well.
>
> A day at Old Court was a red-letter day in many young lives, and I shall never forget how keenly I enjoyed hours spent there, which are amongst the happiest memories of my life.'[337]

There had not been a Waterloo Banquet since the Duke's death in 1852 but small celebrations were held regularly throughout the country by the people who had known or admired him. People would come together to toast the Allied Victory and reminisce about that special time in Britain's history. As Wellington's other friends died over the coming years Georgy became one of the only people left who had been a close friend of the Duke's. Increasingly important figures of the day, including Field-Marshals, Generals and politicians came to visit her. Each Waterloo Day she decorated her downstairs rooms with laurel leaves and lay out all of her mementoes for visitors to see. The miniature of Wellington given to her on the eve of Waterloo took centre stage each time. People who could not make it in person sent beautiful bouquets, baskets of fruit, telegrams and letters.

The 2nd Duke regularly visited Georgy on Waterloo Day. After his death Georgy wrote to Lady Charles Wellesley 'I had known him [the 2nd Duke] all his life, for I was at his & dear Charles's Christening, & they were invariably kind to me. Douro never failed coming to see me till this year...He was always [affectionate] & nice to me...I feel that another link of happy times past is gone & how it is one of the many trials of old age to outlive one's friends.'[338] Georgy and Lady Charles Wellesley continued on good terms over the years, she often sending Georgy a brace of peasants from their shoots at Stratfield Saye. Georgy wrote to her 'I heard the other day that your son Arthur was much interested in any memorials of the Duke. I should be so glad to shew him any I have (for instance the Spanish Prayer book he had in the Peninsula) & to tell him my Waterloo reminiscences.'[339]

Over the years Georgy's sense of duty to Wellington and the history that she had lived through grew. She had many precious objects relating to the Duke, including the Rochard miniature, which were her prized possessions. Another valuable gift the Duke had made to her several years previously had been an incredibly rare sixteenth-century prayer book in Spanish. It was during one of the de Ros family visits to Stratfield Saye that the Duke had alluded to having learnt Spanish from such a book. This book had been particularly precious as it was known to be a rare translation and had been given to him by Lady Elinor Butler and Miss Ponsonby, otherwise known as the Ladies of Llangollen. The two famously eccentric ladies had eschewed mainstream society and lived in isolation together in Wales for over

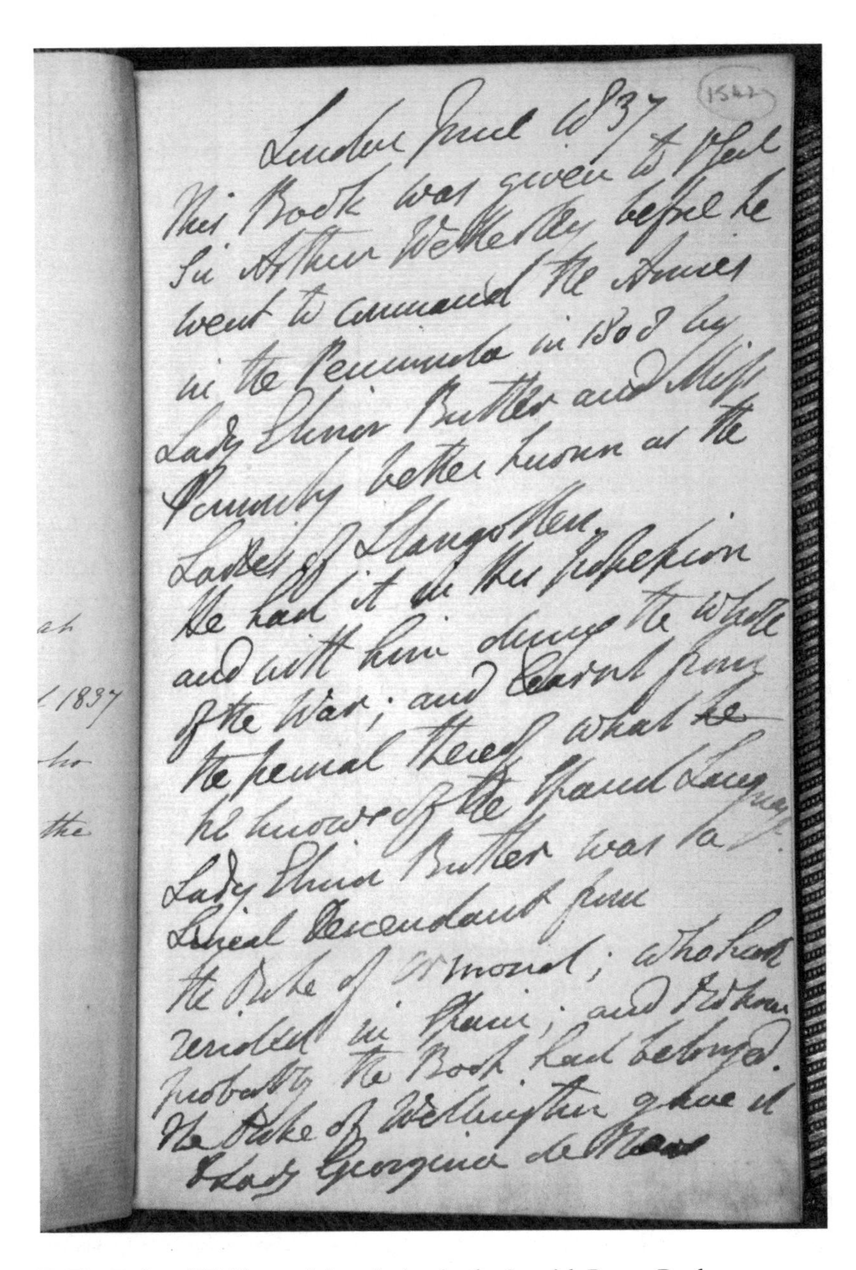

London June 1837
This Book was given to [illegible]
Sir Arthur Wellesley before he
went to command the Armies
in the Peninsula in 1808 by
Lady Eleanor Butler and Miss
Ponsonby better known as the
Ladies of Llangollen.
He had it in his Possession
and with him during the whole
of the War; and learnt from
the perusal thereof what he
knows of the Spanish Language.
Lady Eleanor Butler was a
Lineal Descendant from
the Duke of Ormond; who had
resided in Spain; and to whom
probably the Book had belonged.
The Duke of Wellington gave it
to Lady Georgina de Ros

27. The Duke of Wellington's inscription in the Spanish Prayer Book.

fifty years, welcoming all visitors from Lord Byron to William Wordsworth and Percy Shelley. In 1808, on the way from Ireland to take command of the Peninsular armies, the then Sir Arthur Wellesley had visited the ladies who were friends of the family and they had gifted him this book. The passage to Spain was longer than expected due to bad weather so Wellington had many hours at his leisure to study it. The translation was so accurate that by the time he stepped off the boat he was surprised to understand the whole of the welcome speech addressed to him in Spanish by the principal officer of the port.

When she had been told this story Georgy was intrigued and asked where the prayer book had got to after so many years. The Duke replied 'Oh, it's somewhere in the library here'. Georgy immediately went in search for the book, succeeding after some time in finding it. 'He was very much pleased to see it again, and said he would give it to me, as I had taken such pains to find it.'[340] Soon afterwards Georgy received a letter from the Duke asking for the prayer book back so that he could show it to the Registrar at the University of Oxford. It turned out that this was a very rare translation with perhaps only one or two other copies in existence. Wellington wrote an inscription in the book before he gave it back to Georgy. It ran: 'He [Wellington] had it in his possession and with him during the [Peninsular] war; and learnt from the perusal thereof what he knows of the Spanish language. Lady Elinor Butler was a lineal descendant from the Duke of Ormand, who had resided in Spain, and to whom probably the book had belonged.' It remains perhaps the most valuable and precious Wellington artefact in the de Ros collection. At each Waterloo Day Georgy would get the book out of the case she had carefully sewn for it and show it to friends and family that came to visit. Those that had been too young to know the Duke personally loved seeing his handwritten inscription, alongside Georgy's which noted the date it had been given her as 4th April 1837.

In 1868 Georgy and William took a trip to the undulating plains of Brussels where the Battle of Waterloo had taken place so many years before. Waterloo had been a place of pilgrimage since 1815 and an impressive tourist trade had sprung up selling souvenirs, as well as small objects from the battle which could still being found on the fields. Wellington himself had returned to the battlefield some thirty years previously at the behest of George IV who asked to be taken on a private tour of the battlefield. The Duke had been desperately uncomfortable describing the death and destruction of those days, finally bursting into tears when they reached the spot where Lord Uxbridge had lost his leg. To lose control of his emotions in such an uncharacteristic way showed the long-lasting effect that the battle had had on him. The events of those days had since been retold countless times and by countless people. However, they were not just stories to Wellington, who had lived through the horrors of the battle at close hand and had lost so many friends. School children were already learning about the day having grown up in a world which was largely at peace with its neighbours; a peace that was to be Wellington's greatest legacy.

The aim of Georgy and William's personal trip to Brussels was to search for the ballroom where the ball had taken place the night before the battle. William recorded in his diary 'G. to search out the site of her father's house where the famous ball took place on June 15. 1815. It stood between the Rue Blanchisserie and Boulevard d'Aveers, between Rue du Marais and Rue Neuve but has long been pulled down, the trees in garden shew where it was just opposite Jardin

Botanique.'[341] Although the house was still standing (as it is today), the ballroom had by then already been demolished. Georgy and William walked through the town whilst she told him all that she remembered from those exciting months. These were the streets that had known so much decadence and fun but had also seen such suffering and fear. There were still the ballrooms and theatres where Georgy had taken her first steps into the world as a frivolous youth, worlds apart from the Victorian adulthood she now inhabited. Walking in the park where she had met Wellington with her father the day after the battle, and returning now with William on her arm, how much had changed!

Part of the reason for Georgy's trip was that she was keen to set to rest a debate which had arisen as to the exact location of the Duchess of Richmond's ball. The subject was raised again some years later by Sir William Fraser who asserted that he had found the exact location of the ball room, Georgy was moved to correct him. *The Times* published this report, writing that Georgy was:

> 'not only familiar with all the gallant visitors to her father's house, but was the belle of the ball on that memorable night. Naturally every member of the Duke's staff remembered well Lady Georgiana Lennox. So long as the Duke of Wellington lived he was an intimate personal friend, and almost every other hero of the great fight, and especially those officers and ladies who took part in the dance, continued for many long years within the circle of her acquaintance. Thus Lady de Ros may be said never to have lost touch of Waterloo, and she is convinced the famous ball-room has ceased to exist. Thanks to her marvellous constitution, the Dowager Lady de Ros, the public will be pleased to hear, still preserves in her ninety-third year the complete possession of her bodily and mental faculties...when, more than twenty years ago, Lady de

28. A a portrait engraving of Georgy, by James Rannie Swinton (Blanche's husband). Sadly the original has been lost.

> Ros visited Brussels and examined the locality carefully, she came to the conclusion that the ball-room had stood in the garden behind the Duke's house, and that since then it had been razed.'[342]

Georgy wrote to a friend 'The ball room was not near the size described by Sir W Fraser. It was on the ground floor & not on the 1st floor as described by Sir Wm.'[343] She wrote 'I have been persecuted by correspondence about the Waterloo Ball Room...Twenty years ago I hunted in vain for it, and then heard it had been pulled down long ago, but [they] will not believe me.'[344] As Georgy was one of the few people still alive who had been at the event, she was given the benefit of the doubt.

On 6th January 1874, over twenty years after the Duke of Wellington had died, William and Georgy were finally parted from each other forever; only six months shy of their golden wedding anniversary. William's death was peaceful, after a long and happy life. Lord Dufferin later reflected in a letter to Blanche, 'I never knew two married people who seemed to suit each other so entirely as your father and mother. Your father's lovable qualities, his charming courtesy, his high animal spirits, his simple tastes, his delightful fund of anecdote, were all supplemented and enhanced by the high-bred and refined manners of your mother.'[345] Sadly Georgy's reaction to the loss of the man she had loved for so long has since been lost, but it is easy to imagine.

Dudley, who had retired from the Life Guards two years previously after serving with the regiment for almost thirty years, now succeeded his father as the 24th Baron de Ros. He moved into Old Court with his wife and Georgy moved to London permanently a month later. Although there was plenty of room for her in the big house, or in a cottage on the estate, Georgy did not want to stay in Strangford without William. Georgy moved into the family house in Eaton Place where she continued to enjoy the company of many friends and relations who came to visit her there. But Georgy never returned to Ireland. In the evenings on the rare occasions she was alone she continued to paint beautiful illuminations, as she had done for many years, and knitted shawls for the Distressed Irish Ladies Fund back in Strangford. She particularly adored visits from children, always keeping a stash of bonbons and presents to give to them. She delighted in telling them stories of her youthful adventures with the Duke of Wellington and other leading lights of those early days.

Each year on Waterloo Day Georgy would go to the statue of Wellington as Achilles in Hyde Park and lay a laurel sprig at the feet of her old friend. Georgy, now in her nineties wrote to a friend on one such occasion, 'I had an ovation on Waterloo Day- flowers from many friends, and visits from two field-marshals and four generals! It pleased me that the day should be remembered in these radical times. I am pretty well, only a few small infirmities, but thankful to be as well, as I am bordering on ninety-one!'[346] The following year she wrote 'I was loaded with attentions. Telegrams, letters and such a profusion of flowers, and I had thirty visitors! Among them were five Welles-leys....Altogether I was much gratified at the tribute to my dear old Duke's memory. Would that we had any patriots like him now!'[347] The Queen amongst others would send bouquets on the day. Georgy concluded 'All these attentions gratified me much, as they showed that my dear Duke is not forgotten.'[348]

On one occasion Georgy went to see a public display of Queen Victoria's Jubilee presents including an illumination of her own which she had sent. Soon word spread that old Lady de Ros was there and she was 'at the centre of an admiring circle, who peeped round her eagerly, in order to see her, while she was absorbed in what was before her.'[349] One even whispered 'That's the old lady herself" On the way out Georgy noticed a painting over the mantelpiece depicting the death of the Duke of Brunswick at Waterloo. After examining the picture 'tears ran down her cheeks as she described the scene' to her companion, who saw that 'to her the remembrance of that long past summer morning was as fresh as ever. The London crowd, intent only on getting away as quickly as possible, never noticed the picture that had so profoundly affected her, bringing back to her memory the days of her youth.'[350]

It was not until a few years later that Georgy was given an opportunity to reminisce with another admirer of Wellington's who had known him well: she was invited to take tea with the Queen. Georgy went to the Palace and was 'extremely pleased by the Queen's cordiality and kindness.'[351] The Dowager Duchess of Roxburghe wrote to Dudley afterwards 'I must tell you how delighted the Queen was with your dear and wonderful mother's visit, and I wish you could have heard all Her Majesty said.'[352] Georgy wrote a report of the day to Blanche, 'Nothing could be kinder than H.M. was; embraced me twice, and talked on many subjects. I was tête-à-tête with her for more than twenty minutes; she asked about you, and talked of Dudley. She asked me a good deal about the Duke'.[353]

It is charming to think of the old widowed Queen and the elderly Georgy exchanging stories of their beloved war hero. Certainly

Georgy had many anecdotes to share. Indeed, such was the popularity of the Duke of Wellington and the Battle of Waterloo that the public clamoured for more information about the man and the time. Georgy was persuaded by her family to set about recording her own memories of the days of her youth. As a keen reader herself, she could see the merit in such an exercise, and duly began to collect her favourite memories and anecdotes about the Duke. In the archive in Ireland there are still bundles of Georgy's draft manuscripts, carefully annotated, as she decided how best to tell her story.

She was in her nineties when her *Personal Recollections of the Great Duke of Wellington* were published in *Murray's Magazine.* Georgy was indignant when reviews wrongly praised her work as that 'of an octogenarian' observing 'they might have given me the credit of being a nonagenarian!'[354] However she happily remarked that 'it was not often any one made their debut as an author at the age of ninety-three!'[355] Georgy's recollections proved to be popular and she was thrilled to have set to print her memories in such a way. She received many kind notes of admiration for her work including one from the Marquis of Dufferin and Ava who wrote: 'I have found several people here who have read you articles with the greatest admiration; indeed, anything that concerns the Duke of Wellington cannot fail to interest an Englishman...I envy you your reminiscences.'[356]

Blanche recalled that as well as writing, her mother:

> 'to the last took a keen interest both in public affairs and in the private concerns of her relations and friends...until her sight failed, her handwriting was beautifully clear. Every note and letter was scrupulously answered by herself, and she regularly kept a diary, besides doing all her household and other

> accounts. She was extremely fond of reading, and delighted in being read to. Memoirs and biography were her favourite studies, but she also enjoyed a good novel, whether by Jane Austen or a more modern author.'[357]

She was also a keen embroiderer. The spinning wheel she used had been presented to her by Queen Victoria. Every winter she crocheted a dozen shawls for Christmas presents and she also painted her favourite religious texts into illuminations over the long winter months when the weather often kept her indoors.

Georgy's health was now often bad: 'The severe and sudden changes in the weather have tried me a good deal, but I am not laid up, and I can occupy myself at home, and swarms of nephews and nieces appear most days, so I am very thankful to be as well as I am, thought I have been out very seldom.'[358] In another letter Georgy wrote, 'I am grown deaf and stupid! I have nearly lost the sight in one eye; I trust the other will last my time. I am well, barring a few small ailments, and very thankful to be as well as I am. I had a visit from my great-great granddaughters, which was a great pleasure to me.'[359] 'Aunt Georgy' was beloved of all her extended family who came to see her on a regular basis.

At the close of her ninety-fifth year Georgy was attacked by a severe illness and there was a report in *The Times* on New Year's Eve that she had died. This caused a storm of telegrams and visits to Eaton Place but the report was in error and Georgy was in fact still very much alive. Georgy received the notice of her death and laughed that it was 'the first I had heard of it!'[360] However she was still quite ill, having been confined to her bed for several weeks. She did eventually recover some of her strength and was able to write letters again but did not venture out that winter and by Easter her sight was so bad that she could no longer read or write. She 'felt the privation acutely, but submitted to it most patiently, and after a little she resumed her knitting, and sat herself to work to learn writing with a frame.'[361] The summer months were kinder to her health but in the winter of 1891 she succumbed to a congestion of the lungs. She passed away peacefully and quietly on 15th December surrounded by her family.

Georgy was laid to rest alongside William at the Old Court Chapel and at the same hour a memorial service was held at St. Peter's Church in London's Eaton Square. Both services were packed with family, friends and admirers. She had certainly enjoyed a long and fulfilling life and for those who had known her well, it was difficult to conceive a life without 'Auntie Georgy'. Dudley and Blanche received many touching letters and tributes to their dear mother. Among the many wreaths which were sent to Eaton Place was one from Queen Victoria, herself another old lady whose death a few years later would mark the end of the Victorian era, and the traditions and identities of the nineteenth century.

Lady Georgiana Lennox, later Lady de Ros, was both ordinary and extraordinary. As a young girl she was confident and fun-loving, she enjoyed the romances of adolescence and then went on to marry for love. She was a devoted wife, mother and grandmother. As such her story is not so very different from many other society ladies of her time. But her unique and special friendship with the Duke of Wellington, one of Britain's most revered and celebrated heroes, affords her a very special place in history. There is little doubt that, as time passed, she had a growing sense of her duty to preserve his memory. By the time of her death Georgy was a rare and tangible link to a past where Britain's glory had shone on the battlefields of Waterloo. So much has been documented about the Duke's life and his achievements since that time: dispatches, memorials, biographies and even a roaring trade in the collection of his personal possessions. Georgy's story is different: its universal appeal lies in its retelling of a private and personal friendship that transcends time. It is a story of a great friendship as well as a story of great mutual love and respect. She was, over and above all her other accolades, Wellington's very dearest Georgy.

29. A photograph of Georgy when an old lady, knitting outside Old Court, Strangford. Possibly taken by the Hon. Blanche de Ros, who like her brother was a keen amateur photographer.

EPILOGUE

Georgy's long life spanned an eventful time in British history. In 1809, as a young girl, she witnessed King George III's Jubilee celebrations and seventy-eight years later she watched as Queen Victoria celebrated another Jubilee in Westminster Abbey. But none of these events came close to Georgy's front row seat to the goings on before, during, and after the Battle of Waterloo. Such was the fame of the battle, it gained legendary status within months of its occurrence and its champion, the Duke of Wellington, became not just a hero, but an icon to the British nation.

The world that Georgy left behind was very different to the one she had entered nearly a century before. This was now a world were industry and commerce flowed freely, messages could cross the country in hours not days, and every exploit of the military was reported to the masses through a revolution in the printing press. Georgy had a very powerful sense of duty to preserve not just her memories but also the values of an age which was quickly becoming consumed and overtaken by the modern world. Her writings and retellings of the stories of her youth was all part of this effort to preserve history. Her efforts were appreciated by those who knew and loved her, illustrated in this charming poem which was written by one of her nephews or nieces:

Who from her mine of girlish store
Drew words that made to live one more
The Hero whom we all adore,
And laid Sir William on the floor?
Aunt Georgy!

Who told the tale of Waterloo,
Its Ball, its flight, its Captain too;
And how before the flight Aunt Loo [Louisa]
Put on his sword, as not quite true?
Aunt Georgy!

And who thro' all these long long years
Of joy and sorrow, laughter, tears,
Of radiant hopes, and trembling fears
Won all our hearts? Her name appears!
Aunt Georgy![362]

Georgy preserved as much as she could of her past, possessions and gifts from Wellington and from Queen Victoria as well as letters and notes. Her published recollections show not only a nation's appetite for anything to do with the Great Duke, but also her desire to honour his memory with a true account. Her daughter Blanche was similarly motivated to record the past as two years after Georgy's death she published through John Murray *A Sketch of the Life of Georgiana, Lady de Ros, with Some Reminiscences of her Family.* At the back of this volume Blanche included her mother's Recollections which had been originally published in *Murray's Magazine*. Blanche's account of her mother's life is somewhat selective but useful in that it contains many letters which are no longer in possession of the de Ros family. Filling in the gaps and putting the spice back into Georgy's earlier life has been at times challenging. The Victorians were as passionate about covering up the scandals and affairs of their elders as the Regency bucks had been about conducting them.

In the years following her death and the publication of Blanche's biography Georgy Lennox's name has slipped into obscurity. Her more famous counterparts such as Marianne Patterson, Harriet Arbuthnot and Angela Burdett-Coutts have become the women most associated with the Duke of Wellington. Meanwhile the house at Strangford where Georgy and William had enjoyed so many happy sunny days stood for a further fifty years until it was tragically destroyed by fire. Since then the family has rebuilt in a more modern form and to this day call the estate at Strangford their home. It is an exquisitely beautiful place and it has been a joy to discover Georgy and William's story in the quiet peace of their seaside retreat there.

Georgy's story is one full of colour and sparkle, a life that was privileged but where hardship and heartache were also familiar. Above all, it is the story of a great friendship and how Georgy worked to preserve and promote the memory of her dearest friend, the Duke of Wellington. This book has sought to do the same for Georgy as she did for the Duke – taking letters, keepsakes and possessions, as well as official and unofficial records, to paint a true picture of a wonderful life, and to voice a story well worth telling.

FOOTNOTES

INTRODUCTION & CHAPTER ONE - THE GREAT SIR ARTHUR

1. Farington J., *Diary of Joseph Farington, Vol XII*, p.3027, 20th April 1807, ed. Greig J., London, 1928
2. Hibbert C., *George III, A Personal History*, London, 1998, p.296
3. Lennox WP., *Fifty Years' Biographical Reminiscences*, London,1863, pp.56-7
4. Lennox WP., Vol.I, p.83
5. Swinton B., *A Sketch of the Life of Georgiana, Lady de Ros, with Some Reminiscences of her Family*, London, 1893 p.3, extracts from de Ros G., *Personal Recollections of the Great Duke of Wellington, Part 1, Murray Magazine*, London, 1888
6. Calvert, Ed. Blake W., *An Irish Beauty of the Regency*, London, 1911, pp.66-7, see also Longford Vol. I., pp. 154-5
7. Longford E., *Wellington the Years of the Sword*, London, 1969, p.163
8. Ibid., p.118
9. Ibid., pp.87-8
10. Swinton B., p.122
11. William Ogilvie to his wife Emily, Dowager Duchess of Leinster (the Duke of Richmond's aunt) Dublin 27th October, 1809, as read in Swinton B., pp.4-5
12. Ibid., pp.4-5
13. Ibid., p.8
14. Report of Lord March's condition after injury sustained at the Battle of Orthez
15. Letter from the 1st Duke of Wellington, Orthez 28th July 1814

16. Ibid
17. Letter from the 1st Duke of Wellington on the occasion of Lord March's injury
18. Lennox WP., p.133
19. Millar, D., *The Duchess of Richmond's Ball*, Kent, 2005, p.11

CHAPTER TWO - THE WASH HOUSE

20. Madan S., Spencer and Waterloo Letters: 1814-16, London, 1970, p.95
21. Capel Lady C., Ed. Anglesey, *The Capel Letters: Being the Correspondence of Lady Caroline Capel and Her Daughters with the Dowager Countess of Uxbridge from Brussels and Switzerland 1814-1817,* London, 1955, p.57
22. Ibid., Capel M., pp.68-69
23. Ibid., Capel G., p.62
24. Swinton B., p.124
25. Madan S., pp.23-4
26. Ibid., p.53
27. Ibid., pp.30-31
28. Capel C., p.72
29. Ibid
30. Ibid., p.44
31. Ibid., p.71
32. Ibid
33. Madan S., p.61
34. Ibid
35. Stuart-Wortley V., *Highcliffe and the Stuarts*, London, 1927, p.225
36. Capel C., p.75
37. Capel G., p.76

38. Madan S., p.53
39. Capel H., pp.46-47
40. Capel C., p.45
41. Capel H., p.47
42. Ibid., p.52
43. Lennox WP., p.226
44. Capel C., p.84
45. Madan S., p.40
46. Capel G., p.78
47. Ibid
48. Malmesbury J., *Diaries and Correspondence, Vol II,* London,1816
49. Capel G., p.79
50. 1st Duke of Wellington to Lady Georgiana Lennox, Paris, 3rd January 1817
51. Ibid., Paris, 8th March 1817
52. Swinton B., pp.123-4
53. 1st Duke of Wellington to Lord Bathurst, Despatches., XII.358, London, 1838
54. Longford E., *Wellington the Years of the Sword,* London 1969, p.395
55. Madan S., p.42
56. Capel C., p.102
57. Jackson B, *'Reminiscences'*, see Delaforce P., *Wellington the Beau The Life and Loves of the Duke of Wellington, p.80, Gloucestershire,* 1990, p.80
58. Ibid
59. Swinton B., p.125
60. Capel C., p.102
61. Ibid., p.107

CHAPTER THREE - THE BALL

62. Letter from the 1st Duke of Wellington to John Croker, 8th August 1815, see ed. Sibome H., *The Waterloo Letters*, London, 1891
63. Madan S., pp.102-3
64. Richardson E., *Long Forgotten Days (Leading to Waterloo)*, London 1926, p.373
65. Ibid
66. Millar D., p.69
67. This section of the house was demolished in 1827 to make way for the Rue de Cendres.
68. Stuart-Wortley V., p.235
69. Swinton B., p.128
70. Lennox WP., p.233
71. Swinton B., pp.127-8
72. Ibid., p.136
73. Lennox J., from Millar p. 139
74. Capel C., p.112
75. Richardson E., p.374
76. Letter from Lady Louisa Tighe, 13th January 1889, *The History of the Gordon Highlanders, Vol. I*, p.349
77. Longford E., Vol I., p.508
78. This map was lost or stolen. It never returned from Canada with the Duke of Richmond's other possessions.
79. Story told by Richmond to Captain Bowles two minutes after it occurred. Ed. Malmesbury, *A Series of Letters of the 1st Earl of Malmesbury, His Family and Friends 1745-1820*, London, 1852, Vol II., p.455
80. Swinton B., p.128
81. Ibid., p.137
82. Capel C., p.111

CHAPTER FOUR- WITNESSING WATERLOO

82a. Letter from Lady Sarah Lennox to Lady Georgina Bathurst, 19th June 1815

83. Capel C., p.111

84. Ed. Miller, *Lady de Lancey at Waterloo: A Story of Duty and Devotion*, London, 2007, p.48

85. Eaton, Charlotte Anne [An Englishwoman], *The Days of Battle: or, Quatre Bras and Waterloo, London, 1870* p.24

86. Lady Georgiana Lennox to Lady Bathurst, Brussels, 16th June, 1815

87. Swinton B., p.247

88. Ibid., p.139

89. Lady Georgiana Lennox to Lady Bathurst, Brussels, 16th June 1815

90. Ibid., 17th June 1815

91. Lady Georgiana Lennox to Lady Georgina Bathurst, Brussels, 3rd July 1815

92. Swinton B., p.139

93. Lady Charlotte Greville to Lady Georgina Bathurst, Brussels, 3rd July 1815

94. Swinton B., p.140

95. Ibid., p.138

96. Ibid., p.140

97. Longford E., Vol. I., p.577

98. Ibid., pp. 577-8

99. Ibid., p.579

100. Ibid., p.580

101. Swinton B., p.245

102. Ibid., p.141

103. Ibid

104. Longford E., *Vol. I.*, p.589 The accurate estimate for the loss of Allied lives at Waterloo was between 20-23,000
105. Lord Apsley to his mother, Countess Bathurst, undated.
106. Lady Sarah Lennox to Lady Georgina Bathurst, Brussels, 19th June 1815
107. Lady Charlotte Greville to Lady Georgina Bathurst, Brussels, 3rd July 1815
108. Lady Georgiana Lennox to Lady Georgina Bathurst, Brussels, 22nd June 1815
109. Ibid
110. The hon. Seymour Bathurst to The Earl Bathurst, 22nd June 1815
111. Shelley *Vol. I.*, p.102 see Longford E., Vol I., p. 591
112. Ibid., 3rd July 1815
113. Lady Charlotte Greville to Lady Bathurst, 3rd July 1815
114. Lady Georgiana Lennox to Lady Georgina Bathurst, Brussels, 27th June 1815
115. 1st Duke of Wellington to Lady Georgiana Lennox, Orville, 28th June 1815. One of the miniatures made up by the artist after Waterloo was given to Lady Louisa Lennox, later Lady Tighe, and is now in a private collection.
116. 1st Duke of Wellington Lady Georgiana Lennox, Paris 13th July 1815
117. Lady Georgiana Lennox to Lady Bathurst, 3rd July 1815
118. Ibid., Paris, 14th August 1815. The watercolour by Thomas Heaphy is now in the Goodwood Collection

CHAPTER FIVE- RIDING THE COACH

119. Freemantle J., p.271
120. Madan S., p.163
121. Lady Sarah Lennox to Lady Georgina Bathurst, Brussels, 4th August 1815

122. Ibid
123. Ibid., p.167
124. Ibid., p.166
125. Ibid., pp.157-8
126. Madan S., p.160
127. The 1st Duchess of Wellington, Seaforth Papers: Letters from 1796-1843, pub. Littell's *The Living Age*, 12th December, 1863, p. 494
128. Letter from Rev. GG Somerset to George Trower Esq., 16-17th October 1815, see Millar D., p.187
129. Ibid
130. Ibid., Paris 23rd November, Millar p.190
131. 1st Duke of Wellington to Lady Georgiana Lennox, Paris, 9th January 1816
132. Ibid
133. Ibid
134. Ibid
135. Ibid., Cambray, 6th September 1816
136. Freemantle J., *Cambrai* 17th October 1817, Ed. Glover G., *Wellington's Voice: The Candid Letters of Lieutenant Colonel John Freemantle, Coldstream Guards,* London, 2012, 1808-1821, p.274
137. Swinton B., p.146
138. Ibid
139. Freemantle J., p.274
140. 1st Duke of Wellington to Lady Georgiana Lennox, Mont St. Martin, 17th November 1816
141. Swinton B., p.148
142. Freemantle G., Ed. Glover G., p.248. *Cambrai*, 25th October 1816
143. Swinton B., pp.150-1
144. 1st Duke of Wellington to Lady Georgiana Lennox, Mont St. Martin, 17th November 1816
145. Ibid., 19th December 1816

146. Freemantle J., *Cambrai,* 11th Nov 1816, p.250

146a Letter from Georgiana, Lady de Ros to the Dowager Duchess of Richmond, Goodwood Archive

147. Ibid

148. Georgiana, Lady de Ros to the Dowager Duchess of Richmond, Chomleys c.1840's, Goodwood Archive Ms 383

149. 1st Duke of Wellington to Lady Georgiana Lennox, Paris, 15th January 1817

150. Ibid., 1st February 1817

151. Ibid.

152. Ibid., 1st January 1817

153. Freemantle J., *Paris* 5th February 1817, p.255

154. 1st Duke of Wellington to Lady Georgiana Lennox, Paris, 8th March 1817

155. Ibid., 10th March 1817

156. Freemantle J., *Cambrai* 5th November 1817, pp.276-7

157. Ibid

158. Freemantle J., 7th November 1817, pp.276-7

159. Ibid

160. Ibid., 23rd November 1817, pp.276-7

161. Ibid

162. Ibid

163. Ibid., 26th December 1817, pp.276-7

164. Ibid., 21st July 1818, p.294

CHAPTER SIX - TRAGEDIES & LOVE AFFAIRS

165. Shelley F., Ed. Edgcumbe R., *The diary of Frances Lady Shelley 1787-1873, Vol.I.,* London, 1912, p.75

166. Ed. Cave K., *The Diary of Joseph Farington,* Yale University Press, 1984, Vol. XV, p.5210

167. Lady Louisa Tighe to James C. Stuart, Ireland 10th May 1898, Parliamentary Library, Ottowa, Canada
168. Edgcumbe R. and Shelley F., The Diary of Frances Lady Shelley, Vol II, 1913, pp.77-78
169. Ibid., p.80
170. Account of the 4th Duke of Richmond's last words as scribed by General Bowles
171. Ibid
172. The 1st Duke of Wellington to Lady Georgiana Lennox, Stratfield Saye, 19th October 1819
173. Lady Bathurst to Lady Georgiana Lennox, Wood End, 1819
174. Ibid
175. Bamford F. and Wellington G., *The Journal of Harriet Arbuthnot 1820-32 (Vol II)*, London, 1950, p.417
176. Swinton B., p.18
177. Ed. Pearce E., *The Diaries of Charles Greville*, London, 2006, pp.15-16

CHAPTER SEVEN - BOYLE FARM

178. Horace Walpole to Miss Berry 3rd April 1791, see Melville L., T*he Berry Papers, being the Correspondence of Mary and Agnes Berry 1763-1852*, London, 1914, p.64
179. Public Record Office of Northern Ireland (PRONI), Ref D638/165
180. Baker GM., *Boyle Farm - Thames Ditton, its History and Associations, 1987, ref. Lewis,* XXXV, p.390
181. Ibid., Barrett, vol.II., p.207
182. Ibid., Barrett, p.200
183. Ibid., Barrett, vol. I, p.200
184. Ed. Illchester and Stavordale, *The life and letters of Lady Sarah Lennox, 1745-1826, daughter of Charles, 2nd Duke of Richmond,*

and successively the wife of Sir Thomas Charles Bunbury, bart., and of the Hon. George Napier: also a short political sketch of the years 1760 to 1763 by Henry Fox, 1st Lord Holland, Vol.II., London, 1901, p.115

185. Baker GM., see Manuscripts of J.B. Fortescue, Series 30, vol.VIII, p.185
186. Ibid
187. Ed Stewart AF, *The Diary of a Lady-in-waiting by Charlotte Bury, 1908, vol.I,* London, p.221
188. Ibid., p.169-70
189. Ed. Pearce E., *The Diaries of Charles Greville*, London, 2006, p.30

CHAPTER EIGHT - CONTENTMENT

189a Letter from Lady Pamela Campbell, (neé Fitzgerald) to Miss Emily Eden, see Eden. E.

190. William de Ros diary entry 4th May 1827
191. Ibid., 6th May 1827
192. Bamford F. and Wellington G., *The Journal of Harriet Arbuthnot 1820-32* (Vol I), London, 1950, pp.12-13
193. Lady Campbell to Miss Eden 14th May 1824, Ed. Dickinson V., *Miss Eden's Letters*, London, 1919, p.83
194. Lady Bathurst to Lady Georgiana de Ros, 10th Feb 1824
195. Lady Campbell to Miss Eden, *Miss Eden's letters*, London, 1919, p.84
196. Swinton B., p.15
197. Ed. Uchester, *Elizabeth Holland to her son 1821-1845*, London 1946, p.100
198. Lady Campbell to Miss Eden, June 1824, *Miss Eden's Letters*, London, 1919, p.85
199. Diary of William de Ros, 26th February 1825

200. Ibid., 1826
201. Lady Campbell to Miss Eden, Calne 13 January 1826, *Miss Eden's Letters,* London, 1919, p.99
202. Lady Georgiana de Ros to William de Ros, 28th Monday 1825
203. Swinton B., p.17
204. Ibid
205. William de Ros diary entry 1827
206. Ibid., 1826 review
207. Ibid., 11th March 1827
208. Ibid
209. Ibid., 17th April 1827
210. Letter from Miss Eden to Lady Georgiana de Ros, May 1833
211. Swinton B., p.13
212. Letter from Priscilla, Lady Burghersh to Georgiana, Lady de Ros, Deal Castle, Kent 2nd October 1839
213. Ibid., undated
214. Letter from Miss Eden to Lady Campbell, July 1827, Bigods, Essex, *Miss Eden's Letters,* London, 1919 p.134
215. Ibid
216. Ibid., pp.133-5
217. Ed. Russell J., *Memoirs, Journal and Correspondence of Thomas Moore, 1853-6, Vol.V,* London, 1853, pp.180-2
218. *The Times*, 5th July 1827
219. Letter from Miss Eden to Lady Campbell, *Miss Eden's Letters,* London, 1919, p.145
220. Letter from Lady Bathurst to Georgiana de Ros, 16th December 1825
221. Lady Georgiana de Ros diary entry, 18th June 1836
222. Holmes R., *Wellington: The Iron Duke.* London, 2002, p. 285
223. Swinton B., p.158

223a Ibid., p.159

224. Letter from Charles Artbuthnot to Lady Georgiana de Ros, Walmer Castle, 26th September 1837
225. Letter from the 1st Duke of Wellington to Lady Georgiana de Ros, 23rd June 1832
225a Diary of Georgiana, Lady de Ros
226. Letter from the 1st Duke of Wellington to the Hon. Blanche Fitzgerald-de Ros, Stratfield Saye, 11th February 1838

CHAPTER NINE- ADVENTURES OUT EAST

227. Letter from William de Ros to Lady Georgiana de Ros, 13th August 1834
228. Ibid., 3rd August 1835
229. Ibid., 2nd August 1835
230. Ibid., 10th April 1834
231. Ibid
232. Ibid., 3rd August 1835
233. Ibid., 2nd August 1835
234. Ibid., 13th August, 1834
235. Ibid
236. Ibid
237. de Ros W., p.45
238. Ibid., p.54
239. Letter from William de Ros to Lady Georgiana de Ros, 3rd September 1834
240. de Ros W., p.70
241. Ibid., p.84
242. Ibid., 10th December
243. Ibid
244. Letter from William de Ros to Henry, Lord de Ros, 11th December
245. Letter from William de Ros to Lady Georgiana de Ros, Bucharest

10th December

246. Ibid., 12th December

247. Letter from Lady Bathurst to William de Ros, Steine 12th Feb, 1836

CHAPTER TEN - SCANDAL

247a. Diary of Harriet Arbuthnot, see Bamford F. and Wellington G., *The Journal of Harriet Arbuthnot*

248. Ed. Pearce E., *The Diaries of Charles Greville*, London, 2006, p.154

249. Ibid., p.156

250. Ibid

251. Letter from William de Ros to Lady Georgiana de Ros, 12th Nov 1836

252. 1st Duke of Wellington to Lady Georgiana de Ros, Strafield Saye, 30th November 1836

252a Annual Register for 1837, as read in Foulkes N., *Gentlemen and Blackguards or Gambling Mania and the Plot to steal the Derby of 1844*, London, 2010, p.122

253. Ed. Oman C., *The Gascogyne Heiress The Life and Diaries of Frances Mary Gascoyne-Cecil 1802-39*, London, 1968, p.233

254. Ed. Pearce E., *The Diaries of Charles Greville*, London, 2006, p.157

255. Ibid, pp.158-9

256. Oman C., p. 235

257. Diary of Lady Georgiana de Ros, 2nd September 1838

258. Ibid., 28th June 1838

259. Ibid., 2nd September 1838

260. Letter from Lady Georgiana de Ros to William de Ros, Stratfield Saye Tuesday 26th March, 1839

261. Ibid
262. Diary of Queen Victoria, Saturday 26th January 1839, Lord Esher transcript, p.266, The Royal Collection
263. Letter from Lady Georgiana de Ros to William de Ros, Stratfield Saye, 26th March 1839
264. Swinton B., p.29
265. Ibid
266. 1st Duke of Wellington to Georgiana, Lady de Ros, Strafield Saye, December 1837
267. Ibid., 31st May 1838

CHAPTER ELEVEN - REMEMBRANCE

268. Ibid., Walmer Castle 18th October, 1839, see Swinton B., pp.163-4
269. Ibid., 28th November, 1838
270. Ibid., Walmer Castle 7th Oct 1837
271. Ibid., 25th March 1838
272. Ibid., 28th November, 1838
273. Ibid
274. Ibid., Stratfield Saye, 25th February 1838
275. Ed. Wellington G., *Wellington and his Friends*, London, 1965, p.242
276. Letter from Charles Arbuthnot to Georgiana, Lady de Ros, Walmer Castle, 26th September 1837
277. Ibid
278. The 1st Duke of Wellington to Angela Burdett-Coutts, London 4th September 1848, *Wellington and his Friends, Letters of the First Duke Selected and edited by the Seventh Duke of Wellington*, London and New York, 1965, p.264.
279. 'Inventory of Dyce Sombre's effects' 9th August 1845, L/L/65, (145), British Library, see also Fisher M., *The Inordinately Strange life of Dyce Sombre Victorian Anglo-Indian MP and Chancery*

'Lunatic', London, 2010, p.148

280. Ibid., p.149
281. Letter from 1st Duke of Wellington to Georgiana, Lady de Ros, London 17th March 1838
282. Ibid., 25th March 1838
283. Ibid., 31st May 1838
284. Ibid., 14th June 1838
285. Diary of Miss Jervis, see *The Inordinately Strange life of Dyce Sombre Victorian Anglo-Indian MP and Chancery 'Lunatic'*, London, 2010, p.149

285a. Letter from the 1st Duke of Wellington to Georgiana, Lady de Ros, 11th August 1838

286. Ibid., Walmer Castle, 9th September 1838
287. Ibid., 19th October 1838
288. Ibid
289. Ibid., Walmer Castle 6th November 1838
290. Ibid., Stratfield Saye 7th Jan 1841
291. Letter from 1st Duke of Wellington to Georgiana, Lady de Ros, London, 9th February 1840
292. Ibid., 9th February1840
293. Ibid., Stratfield Saye 11th February 1838
294. Ibid., 25th February 1838
295. Ibid., London 17th March 1838
296. Priscilla, Lady Burghersh to Georgiana, Lady de Ros, 19th February 1842
297. Georgina, Lady de Ros, diary Walmer Castle 14th September 1842
298. Lady Georgina Bathurst to Georgiana, Lady de Ros, 15th September 1852
299. The 1st Duke's valet Kendall to Georgiana, Lady de Ros, 14th February [1840?]
300. Ibid., 20th Feb 1840
301. Priscilla, Lady Burghersh to Georgiana, Lady de Ros, London 19th

February 1842

302. Diary of Georgiana, Lady de Ros, 5th April 1847
303. Ibid., 9th April 1847
304. Letter from the Hon. Frances de Ros to Georgiana, Lady de Ros, 21st June 1842
305. The Hon. Frances de Ros to Georgiana, Lady de Ros, undated
306. Swinton B., p.29
307. Georgiana, Lady de Ros to the Dowager Duchess of Richmond, Chomleys c.1840's, Goodwood Archive Mss 383
308. Letter from William, Lord de Ros to Edward Campbell, London 24th February 1851
309. Ibid
310. Ibid
311. Letter from Edward Fitzgerald Campbell, 8th April 1851
312. Letter from the hon. Blanche de Ros to Edward Fitzgerald Aix la Chapelle 17th June 1852
313. Diary of Georgiana, Lady de Ros, 3rd February 1852
314. Ibid., 23rd February 1852

314a Diary of William, Lord de Ros, 1951

315. Undated letter from William, Lord de Ros to Edward Campbell, c.February 1852
316. Ibid
317. Diary of William, Lord de Ros, 11th November 1852
318. Diary of Georgiana, Lady de Ros, 7th June 1852. Blanche dried this bouquet and kept it for many years.
319. Ibid., 16th June 1852
320. The 1st Duke of Wellington's valet Kendall to Georgiana, Lady de Ros, Walmer Castle, 14th September 1852
321. Ibid., Walmer Castle 14th September 1852
322. Diary of Georgiana, Lady de Ros, 17th September 1852
323. Diary of William, Lord de Ros, 17th September 1852

324. 2nd Duke of Wellington to William, Lord de Ros, September 1852
325. Priscilla, Lady Burghersh to Georgiana, Lady de Ros, Vienna 5th October 1852
326. Ibid., 15th September 1852
326a Letter from Lady Georgina Bathurst to Georgiana, Lady de Ros, November 1852
327. Swinton B., p.50
328. Wilson H., *Memoirs*, 2:609
329. Diary of William, Lord de Ros, 18th November 1853
330. Lady Georgina Bathurst to Georgiana, Lady de Ros, 18th November 1852
331. Greville papers 6: 370
332. Swinton B., p.52
333. Ibid., pp.51-52
334. The Duke of Cambridge to William, Lord de Ros, 20th November 1852, St. James's Palace, see Swinton B., pp.52-3
335. Fraser W., *Words on Wellington, The Duke-Waterloo-The Ball*, London, 1889, p.89

CHAPTER TWELVE - REMINISCENCES

336. Swinton B., p.107
337. Swinton B., pp.70-3
338. Georgiana, Dowager Lady de Ros to Lady Charles Wellesley, 20th August 1884, by kind permission of his Grace the 9th Duke of Wellington, from the Wellington collection at Stratfield Saye
339. Ibid., 25th November 1885
340. Swinton B., pp.154-5
341. Diary of William, Lord de Ros, 13th May 1868
342. *The Times* 28th August 1888, article entitled 'The Waterloo Ball Room/It does not exist'

343. Letter from Georgiana, Dowager Lady de Ros to Lady Walsh 4th October, 1883
344. Ibid
345. Letter from the Marquis of Dufferin and Ava to the Hon. Mrs Blanche Swinton, British Embassy Paris, 7th November, 1892
346. Letter from Georgiana, Dowager Lady de Ros to the Hon. Mrs Ward, 20th June 1886
347. Ibid., 20th June, 1889
348. Letter from Georgiana, Dowager Lady de Ros to Lord George Fitzgerald, 9th July 1890
349. Ibid., p.89
350. Ibid., p.90
351. Ibid
352. Letter from the Dowager Duchess of Roxburghe to Dudley, Lord de Ros, see Swinton B., pp.93-4
353. Swinton B., p.94
354. Ibid., p.92
355. Ibid
356. Letter from the Marquis of Dufferin and Ava to Georgiana, Dowager Lady de Ros, 17th March 1889
357. Ibid., pp.82-3
358. Letter from Georgiana, Dowager Lady de Ros to the Hon. Mrs Ward, 29th March 1882
359. Letter from Georgiana, Dowager Lady de Ros to Lady Walsh 4th October 1883
360. Swinton B., p.110
361. Ibid., p.111

EPILOGUE

362. Poem composed by a member of the extended de Ros family

ILLUSTRATIONS

Unless otherwise stated, all images were taken at Old Court, Strangford, by Alice Achache. Copyright retained. Artist and date stated where known.

1. Molecomb House on the Goodwood estate where Georgy and her siblings spent their early years. Image author's own.

2. Cariacture of the 1st Duke of Wellington telling off Georgy's brother William Pitt Lennox, a sketch for his published reminiscences of life as a Lennox. © Tate Britain, London

3. The Château d'Hougoumont, a photograph taken when Georgy and William later visited the site where the Battle of Waterloo had taken place.

4. Hand painted illumination by Georgiana, Lady de Ros. Based on The Book of Hours, a devotional manuscript from the Middle Ages

5. A miniature of Georgy's mother, Charlotte Lennox, 4th Duchess of Richmond.

6. Georgy's father, Lord Charles Lennox, later 4th Duke of Richmond, by Henry Collen after John Hoppner, 1823. © The Trustees of the Goodwood Collection

7. Sir Arthur Wellesley, 1804-5, by Robert Home. A three quarter length version of the original full length, which is in the Royal Collection. This version is owned by the Wellington Family and hangs at Apsley House. © Stratfield Saye Preservation Trust

8. A portrait miniature traditionally known as Lady Georgiana Lennox, who was always called Georgy by her friends.

9. A portrait miniature of Sir Arthur Wellesley, by Richard Cosway R.A, 1808. © Victoria and Albert Museum, London.

10. A miniature of the 1st Duke of Wellington, 1815. This is the miniature given to Lady Georgiana Lennox on the eve of the Battle of Waterloo. On the back is inscribed in Georgy's handwriting 'This miniature is an original and was given to me by the Duke of Wellington at Brussels on 15 June 1815 [signed] 'Georgiana de Ros'. This miniature is now in a private collection in New York. A copy is in the de Ros family collection.

11. A watercolour of the site of Lord Hay's burial at Waterloo, painted by Georgy after her marriage.

12. The Duchess of Richmond's Ball on the 15th June 1815, by Robert Alexander Hillingsford. © The Trustees of the Goodwood Collection

13. Part of the silver service given to Lady Georgiana de Ros by the 1st Duke of Wellington on the occasion of her marriage in 1824.

14. 1st Duke of Wellington, a miniature on enamel by William Essex, after Sir Thomas Lawrence, 1838

15. A miniature of Lady Georgiana de Ros, 1832

16. A hand annotated drawing by Georgy and her siblings, showing the exact location of their mother's ball on 15th June 1815.

17. A photograph taken by Dudley of (left-right) Dudley's wife Mary, Lady Georgiana de Ros, and the Hon. Blanche de Ros, 1858. Acquired by Queen Victoria. Royal Collection Trust/© Her Majesty Queen Elizabeth II 2016

18. A portrait of Georgy by her mother-in-law, Charlotte, Lady de Ros

19. Dudley Fitzgerald-de Ros as a young boy, 1840

20. William Fitzgerald-de Ros, c.1840

21. Georgy in later years, a chalk sketch by Countess Feodora Gleichen, 1871

22. Dudley when 24th Baron de Ros, in his 'Spy' Vanity Fair portrait, entitled 'The Premier Baron'.

23. Large miniature on ivory by Robert Thorburn of the 1st Duke of Wellington with four of his grandchildren in the library at Stratfield Saye, 1852. © Stratfield Saye Preservation Trust

24. The family vault at the chapel at Old Court, Strangford, where Georgy and William are buried. © Paul Flanagan.

25. Another religious illumination by Georgiana, Lady de Ros

26. Strangford, where Georgy and William spent many happy years together with their family.

27. The Duke of Wellington's inscription in the Spanish Prayer Book

28. A a portrait engraving of Georgy, by James Rannie Swinton (Blanche's husband). Sadly the original has been lost.

29. A photograph of Georgy when an old lady, knitting outside Old Court, Strangford. Possibly taken by the Hon. Blanche de Ros, who like her brother was a keen amateur photographer.

COVER ILLUSTRATIONS

Front Cover: See illustration 8, 12 and 27.

Interior: Two more religious illuminations by Georgiana, Lady de Ros

Authors image by Amelia Kosminsky

SELECT BIBLIOGRAPHY

Unless noted, all letters are from the Fitzgerald- de Ros archive. These are available at the Public Record Office of Northern Ireland (PRONI).

For the history of Boyle Farm and Thames Ditton, see Baker GM., *Boyle Farm - Thames Ditton, its History and Associations,* 1987, which is no longer in print but is available online.

The Richmond family archive is held at the West Sussex Record office. The Wellington family archive is held at Stratfield Saye, Hampshire. The diaries of Queen Victoria are held at the Royal Archives and can be accessed online.

Ed. Anglesey, *The Capel Letters: Being the Correspondence of Lady Caroline Capel and Her Daughters with the Dowager Countess of Uxbridge from Brussels and Switzerland 1814-1817,* London, 1955

Bamford F. and Wellington G., *The Journal of Harriet Arbuthnot 1820-32 (Vol II)*, London, 1950

Calvert, Ed. Blake W., *An Irish Beauty of the Regency,* London, 1911

Delaforce P., *Wellington the Beau The Life and Loves of the Duke of Wellington*, Gloucestershire, 1990

Ed. Dickinson V., *Miss Eden's Letters*, London, 1919

de Ros G., *Personal Recollections of the Great Duke of Wellington, Part 1*, Murray Magazine, London, 1888

de Ros W., *Journal of a Tour in the Principalities Crimea and Countries Adjacent to the Black Sea in the Years 1835-36*, London, 1855

Eaton CA [An Englishwoman], *The Days of Battle: or, Quatre Bras and Waterloo*, London, 1870

Edgcumbe R. and Shelley F., *The Diary of Frances Lady Shelley, Vol II*, 1913, pp.77-78 for full account

Farington J., *Diary of Joseph Farington, Vol XII*, p.3027, 20th April 1807, ed. Greig J., London, 1928

Fisher M., *The Inordinately Strange life of Dyce Sombre Victorian Anglo-Indian MP and Chancery 'Lunatic'*, London, 2010

Foulkes N., *Gentlemen and Blackguards or Gambling Mania and the Plot to steal the Derby of 1844*, London, 2010

Fraser, *Words on Wellington, The Duke-Waterloo-The Ball*, London, 1889

Freemantle J., Cambrai 17th October 1817, Ed. Glover G., *Wellington's Voice: The Candid Letters of Lieutenant Colonel John Freemantle, Coldstream Guards*, London, 2012, 1808-1821

Hibbert C., George III, *A Personal History*, London, 1998

Holmes R., *Wellington: The Iron Duke*. London, 2002

Ed. Illchester and Stavordale, *The life and letters of Lady Sarah Lennox, 1745-1826, daughter of Charles, 2nd Duke of Richmond, and successively the wife of Sir Thomas Charles Bunbury, bart., and of the*

Hon. George Napier: also a short political sketch of the years 1760 to 1763 by Henry Fox, 1st Lord Holland, Vol.II., London, 1901

Lennox WP., *Fifty Years' Biographical Reminiscences, Vol.I &II.*, London, 1863

Longford E., *Wellington the Years of the Sword*, London 1969

Longford E., *Wellington Pillar of State*, London, 1972

Madan S., *Spencer and Waterloo Letters: 1814-16*, London, 1970

Ed. Malmesbury, *A Series of Letters of the 1st Earl of Malmesbury, His Family and Friends1745-1820, Vol II*, London, 1852

Malmesbury J., *Diaries and Correspondence, Vol II*, London, 1816

Melville L., *The Berry Papers, being the Correspondence of Mary and Agnes Berry 1763-1852*, London, 1914

Ed. Miller, *Lady de Lancey at Waterloo: A Story of Duty and Devotion*, London, 2007

Ed Stewart AF, *The Diary of a Lady-in-waiting by Charlotte Bury, Vol.I*, London, 1908

Ed. Pearce E., *The Diaries of Charles Greville*, London, 2006

Ed. Oman C., *The Gascogyne Heiress The Life and Diaries of Frances Mary Gascoyne-Cecil 1802-39*, London, 1968

Richardson E., *Long Forgotten Days (Leading to Waterloo)*, London, 1926

Ed. Russell J., *Memoirs, Journal and Correspondence of Thomas Moore, 1853-6, Vol.V*, London, 1853

Shelley F., Ed. Edgcumbe R., *The diary of Frances Lady Shelley 1787-1873, Vol.I.*, London, 1912

Stuart-Wortley V., *Highcliffe and the Stuarts*, London, 1927

Swinton B., *A Sketch of the Life of Georgiana, Lady de Ros, with Some Reminiscences of her Family*, London, 1893

Tillyard S., *Citizen Lord, The Life of Edward Fitzgerald Irish Revolutionary*, New York, 1997

Ed. Uchester, *Elizabeth Holland to her son 1821-1845*, London, 1946

Wellesley C., *Wellington Portrayed*, London, 2014

Ed. Wellington, *Wellington and his Friends, Letters of the First Duke Selected and edited by the Seventh Duke of Wellington*, London and New York, 1965, p.264.

Wilson J., *A Soldier's Wife, Wellington's Marriage*, London, 1987

INDEX

ACKNOWLEDGMENTS

I started work for this book at the age of twenty-two whilst researching portraits of the 1st Duke of Wellington for a catalogue published by the Wellington family. One telephone call later and Georgy Lennox's descendent Peter had offered me full use of his archive to write the biography. Having never met me and without knowing if I could even write, he put his full trust in me. I am fully indebted to Peter and Sian Maxwell for welcoming me so regularly to their beautiful home in Strangford, and for giving me the opportunity to tell Georgy's story.

His Grace the 9th Duke of Wellington gave me my introduction into the world of the 1st Duke and allowed me to use letter extracts and images in the book, for which I thank him. Furthermore, Jane Branfield, the Duke's archivist at Stratfield Saye, has been an invaluable support and provided me with much advice over the last four years. She read early and late chapter drafts and always steered me in the right direction, for which I am eternally grateful.

Alice Achache took most of the wonderful images which illustrate the book and has been a great friend and support over the years. We went on many adventures together, in the name of Wellington and Georgy, of which I will always have happy memories. I also thank Amelia Kosminsky who took the authors image.

Additionally, I am grateful for the support of Josephine Oxley, Keeper of the Wellington Collection at Apsley House. The West Sussex Record Archive was extremely helpful in finding relevant documents for me as were staff at the British Library and the Heinz Archive at the National Portrait Gallery; namely Paul Cox. I also thank James Peill, Curator of the Goodwood Collection, and Rosemary Baird, emeritus Curator of the Goodwood Collection, who answered several of my questions and kindly allowed me to reproduce the beautiful portrait of the Duchess of Richmond's Ball.

I thank Lord Strathcarron and Hugh Tempest Radford at Universe Press for their support of this project over the years and particularly to Lord Strathcarron for his commitment in getting this book to print. Lucie Skilton was my invaluable editor, she worked tirelessly to get the book up to scratch and was a joy to work with. I also thank Lucy Duckworth, Simon Perks, Ryan Gearing, Maisie Franklin and Felicity Price-Smith of Universe Press. My excellent book designer was Maisie Franklin. I am also grateful to my publicist Helen McCuster and also Aimee Coveney for their help in promoting the book.

Several people made the publication of this book possible through their financial support. Special thanks go to Richard Baron Cohen for his wonderful generosity, and also: Joanna Cooper, William Cooper, Christopher Crossland, Emma Crossland, Peter Crossland, Vicki Crossland, Michael Ethelston, Alan Forshaw, Catherine Forshaw, Moira Forshaw, Rachel Harding, Suzy Hickmet, Ed Kitchingman, John MacKenzie, Sophie MacKenzie, Jacob MacKenzie, Oscar Nyman, Marcus Ridge, Emma Ruttle, and Jane Williams.

Alice Marie Crossland

London, July 2016